Clover Garden

Clover Garden

A Carolinian's Piedmont Memoir

BLAND SIMPSON

Photographs by ANN CARY SIMPSON

THE UNIVERSITY OF NORTH CAROLINA PRESS Chapel Hill

This book was published with the assistance of the William R. Kenan Jr. Fund of the University of North Carolina Press.

Designed by Richard Hendel
Set in Quadraat and Scala Sans by codeMantra

Cover photograph by Ann Cary Simpson.

Library of Congress Cataloging-in-Publication Data
Names: Simpson, Bland, author. | Simpson, Ann Cary, photographer (expression)
Title: Clover Garden : a Carolinian's Piedmont memoir / Bland Simpson ;
photographs by Ann Cary Simpson.
Description: Chapel Hill : The University of North Carolina Press, [2024] |
Includes index.
Identifiers: LCCN 2024023921 | ISBN 9781469682891 (cloth ; alk. paper) |
ISBN 9781469682907 (epub) | ISBN 9781469682914 (pdf)
Subjects: LCSH: Simpson, Bland. | Authors—Biography—Anecdotes. | Piedmonts
(Geology)—North Carolina—Social life and customs. | Orange County (NC)—Social
life and customs. | BISAC: NATURE / Regional | HISTORY / United States / State &
Local / South (AL, AR, FL, GA, KY, LA, MS, NC, SC, TN, VA, WV) |
LCGFT: Autobiographies. | Illustrated works.
Classification: LCC F262.07 S56 2024 | DDC 975.6/5—dc23/eng/20240611
LC record available at https://lccn.loc.gov/2024023921

Title page: Shed in afternoon fog, Clover Garden

To the people of Clover Garden

and southwestern Orange

County, North Carolina

A human community, then, if it is to last long, must exert a sort of centripetal force, holding local soil and local memory in place.

—Wendell Berry, *The Work of Local Culture*

Everything fulfills a purpose that is not its own; the hailstone is a journeyman of God; the grass blade carries the universe upon its point.

—William Butler Yeats, *Letters to the New Island*

Bellwort

Contents

Piedmont, North Carolina

Between the big farm, forest, swamp, sound country, and seacoast of North Carolina's broad, flat eastern terraces and the majestic mountain rise we call not *a* but *the* Blue Ridge lie our foothills, the Piedmont: 250 miles of steadily rolling, constantly climbing, long-settled lands covering almost half the east-west distance of our state, with just over 1,000 feet of elevational lift from Rocky Mount's 85 feet at the fall line, where the foothills begin, to Morganton's nearly 1,200 feet in the shadow of that grand, blue-hued ridge, where the Piedmont simply stops like oxen at a barbed wire fence and yields, as it must, to the overpowering heights of the Southern Appalachians.

Fifty years ago someone tried to rename this Piedmont region *the Midlands*, as if we were somehow magically off in England, yet we descendants of the Scots, Scotch-Irish, African Americans, Pennsylvania Dutch, and, too, Native Americans and English, not a one of us would have it, and so no one but the lone person who wrote that puffery for a bank's brochure ever used the phrase.

Piedmont: we are not alone in holding such a landform, as Italy has its grape-growing Piemonte to its northwest, Colorado has a narrow piedmont squeezed between the Great Plains and the Rockies, Alaska's Malaspina has the honor of being the largest piedmont glacier in the world, and the glaciated piedmont under Olympus Mons on Mars is four times the size of Malaspina. Yet North Carolina's Piedmont is among the largest in the country, has a growing season of half to two-thirds of the year, and sits between the broad latitudinal lines where northern and southern flora and fauna overlap (*crossroads of the natural world*, Tom Earnhardt calls it), our lands and woods and waters presenting an incredible melding of natural diversity.

Only three spectacular pieces of topography astonish the simplicity of all this rolling land: the Sauratown Mountains and their Hanging Rock northwest of Greensboro; Pilot Mountain, the monadnock above Winston-Salem seen for miles in any direction; and the Uwharrie Mountains below Asheboro with their near-thousand-foot peaks—all relict rises left in place after

Piedmont waters worked for untold millennia and wore down everything else around them.

Yet all in all, this is plenty, more than enough—elbow room (well, perhaps not enough for Daniel Boone, who left from Hillsborough, western edge of the Carolina frontier, and could not stop till he had had what he wanted of the valleys of the Yadkin and New Rivers and at last reached Kentucky, but enough for the rest of us) and fertile country not so very far outside of only a few big cities and their myriad platted neighborhoods, real honest-to-God oak and hickory and pine forests and red-clay farms—and, to hail in voices both smooth and hoarse this gorgeous green territory, here come string-band music and Piedmont blues all our people's own, with tunes and songs telling the tales of this place, resounding from way back when and sounding out proudly now: the upbeat melancholy of Etta Baker's "One Dime Blues," the fierce and constant blood-pull of home in Mipso's "Carolina Calling Me," the tragedy of our beloved Doc Watson's ghostly tenor in "Omie Wise," and The Red Clay Ramblers' unabashedly celebratory here's-to-down-home "The North Carolina Toast and Breakdown."

And a thousand more songs beyond these.

And another thousand more *before* these, songs we likely will never know sung in languages no longer spoken or heard, accompanied from Time immemorial in these hilly forests and low riverbanks by shell-shakers and cane flutists, well before any Europeans or Africans ever landed and found the far inland and first saw this terrain, this Piedmont—for the Native Americans had already been here at least 12,000 years.

The young English adventurer John Lawson, thinking in early 1701 that he was the first European to curve up through this Carolina territory (not knowing the Spanish had forded and forged west on through to Linville Gorge 130-odd years earlier, or that he would meet more like him before his months-long, lazy-C, on-foot Piedmont tramping was done), did with the help of the Indians trek through modern Alamance and Orange Counties, and he wrote of "Indian Plantations" and "Indian Corn-fields" and bore witness to Native agriculture. And Lawson would see and somehow come to know that the natural fecundity hereabouts—within a huge area just northeast of the Haw, from what is now Saxapahaw much of the way to Hillsborough, which he described as "20 Miles of such extraordinary rich Land, lying all together"—had been providing for the Indigenous peoples for a very, very long time, and the men, women, and children who followed Lawson (because he wrote an appeal to them, telling them about all this richness in his 1709 *New Voyage to Carolina* report) thirty years later into this same big Piedmont agrarian arena gave it a name, or simply learned the Sissipa-haw Indians' name the territory already had and translated it into English, acknowledging the Native farmers and their 600 generations of forebears (who all that time had kept an unwritten compact with the land: to use it but not use it up) with three words leading deep back into the long-disappeared mists of Time and into an antiquity predating even Time itself, their name in English that stuck and told a story of the long-ago, which said it all:

The Old Fields. The Haw or Saxapahaw Old Fields.

The Old Fields where we live.

Clover Garden

PART 1 ❀ *Clover Garden*

Clover Garden is a small, four-square-mile country community in the old Porter Tract of the lower Old Fields, lying beside the Haw River just a few miles west of Chapel Hill and Carrboro, North Carolina: patches of contoured red-clay furrows in southwest Orange County in the state's foothills, growing corn and soybeans and hay and winter wheat, though once also cotton and tobacco, alongside dairy cows, beeves, and horses in pastures meeting deep forests of white oaks and red oaks and pines, copses of them around country churches, and straight-up tulip poplars and high-crown hickories, American beech and always sweet gum, muscadine vines everywhere, willows close to the waterlines of ponds where big blue herons stalk and hunt, ponds full of bass and bream, shellcrackers and punkinseed and catfish prowling the bottoms, and dogwood and redbud fringing the woods with white and a pinkish lavender in early spring—all the waters of these lands draining away (often just after the rains have revealed Indian points and potsherds in our gardens, ironic unintended gifts of the Natives, the first peoples) into the dendritic headwaters of the Cape Fear River and, after flowing 200 miles, out past Oak Island and Bald Head to Frying Pan Shoals where Long Bay and Onslow Bay meet and form the Atlantic Ocean.

Hayfields, Cane Creek valley

Brahmans

Barred owls cry out in the dimming evenings, as heartily as hawks and crows do in the day, Canada geese go honking by, wood ducks and doves noisily winging over the fields too, blue herons flying singly or even in formations of four, bound from Cane Creek to some farm pond and back again. The milk cows here are mostly black-and-white Holstein-Friesians, a German breed, which our children call "two-tones," and sometimes Ayrshires and doe-eyed Jerseys. As dairies (which succeeded the small cotton and tobacco farms run by Blacks and whites alike, those farmers having long since moved on) have closed over time, vines climbing their silos, beef cattle have moved into many a field: Angus, Hereford, Limousin, Charolais. And, lately, even a rescue herd of Brahman cattle have come to live out their days in the heart of the community.

There is no poverty in our nomenclature, for in Clover Garden we are living in the Indians' old-fields realm already agrarian and bountiful when John Lawson saw it, and the native Sissipahaw who farmed and fished here gave their name to the Haw River, running just to our south. The Morrows, early eighteenth-century grantees, gave theirs to the nearby grinding mill on Cane Creek. The Lloyds gave theirs to the small settlement of Lloydtown on a broad flat just north of that mill. And clover, the sweet legume that feeds much of the world, gave its name to this garden spot and to a small chapel and to a post office at the crest of a rise with a long view off and away to the south. A post office opened here under President Thomas Jefferson and closed by the Civil War, no one darkening its door or collecting or mailing a letter there in 160 years, were there even any longer a post office door to darken.

And so, even yet, its name endures: Clover Garden. The chapel, the road, the communion of souls.

To be a citizen of Clover Garden here in the Old Fields, to be a part of its membership, has been and remains a great wonder in my life, and what follows are stories from within that wonder, some of them at least, as I have seen them go down and heard them told: of hounds belling in the night,

Collins Creek, dry bed

of turkeys slowly crossing our little field and of a family of golden skunks drifting as one down the slope of our woods, of cattle out of their fencing and parading up the road at midnight, of hay setting itself afire in a barn, of bonfires climbing high into the New Year's nights, of young men and old stepping and slipping over creek-bed stones at Eastertide in search of suckerfish, of women young and old turning and shaping pots on wheels in the deep woods or quilting old patterns or designs out of their own minds, and of men and women treading the forested lanes together in all seasons, scouting, as one old man called it, seeking and finding the simple pleasures of being out as dusky dark settles over the land, all out in the gloaming to see, through the years, what is moving and what is not.

Those whom we know and have known in this countryside have found many a blessing out here, watching standing deer and deer watching them right back, have counted those blessings, and then quitting their counts only when the numbers just got too high and those blessings, having found us, then dispersed, floating up into the crowns of tulip poplars and loblollies and beyond, into the clouds that course over us from west and southwest and on above them into the bright and timeless evening stars and the planets Venus and Jupiter and Saturn and Mars and the mythic shapes that are real beings to us, Orion and Scorpio and the Big and Little Dippers and every other creation in the true wild blue yonder, from a distance so endless and divine we shall never know it, rolling across our skies every single night in the endless scroll of years.

Cabin Life

At first I lived in a log cabin, or rather a log cabin and a log tobacco barn conjoined by the masterful house carpenter Karl Kachergis and set a scant fifty feet from Cane Creek, not even a mile downstream of the old Morrow Mill. The Schoplers, Eric and Miggie, heroic and oft-traveling international leaders in the world of autism analysis, teaching, and care, had asked Karl to build the cabin on their farm, Beechwood, to house someone like a watchkeeper, someone to be there during the many periods when they were away.

And so I came to this charmed spot, right after doing over 200 performances playing a railroad conductor, a hapless banker, and a conspiring governor in Jim Wann's and my Diamond Studs, our Chapel Hill troupe's original Off-Broadway musical about Jesse James in 1975. I had come straight back home to North Carolina to write and conjure up some more music, theater, and tales and by Christmas of that year was living happily in the Schoplers' cabin in the woods—to say nothing at all against New York City, which has long been good to our thespian tribe—a place about as far away in mode, spirit, and style from the Westside Theatre at Ninth Avenue and Forty-Third Street in the heart of Hell's Kitchen as one might get.

My old friend and mentor Jake Mills, who dearly loved wild North Carolina both afloat and afield and who was a great fisherman and wing shot as well as a world-renowned Spenserian, Renaissance scholar, and teacher, came out, took one look at the place, and passed judgment: "You have now certifiably gotten yourself way out yonder where there ain't nobody never is!"

My dear mother—who grew up in Chapel Hill in the 1920s and 1930s (and even saw President Roosevelt at Woollen Gym when he came to the university) and lived there most of her life—thought I had somehow reneged on being a lifelong town resident and had now moved to the absolute ends of the earth. She and her mother (Evelyn, born way out in Alligator, North Carolina, in eastern Tyrrell County) both would always refer to particularly slackly dressed country folk who reminded them of swamp timber-camp dwellers as "looking like something that had *come in from the Nine-Miles.*"

Now, with my new location and my brown Australian floppy hat, I had become a Nine-Miles man.

To the cabin within a week or so of my moving in, December 1975, my bright, witty UNC *Law Review* sister, Susie, helped me, with the aid of some Hall's Creek General Store baling twine, tie onto the car roof a fourteen-foot loblolly pine and bring it back from the woods down on Big Flatty Creek in Pasquotank County in the Albemarle, the tree fitting nicely beneath the high-vaulted ceiling and making the new place ready for Christmas that year.

In that front room, with its hearthstones and huge fieldstone fireplace, another great friend, Union Grove champion old-time banjoist Tommy Thompson—cofounder of The Red Clay Ramblers—and I often played music together. Tommy was well acquainted with any number of folk musicians he called "old-timers," men of both races, and knew southern banjo and fiddle artistry very well indeed, from playing with Tommy Jarrell of Toast, North Carolina, and clawhammering Dink Roberts of Haw River and Joe and Odell Thompson also of Alamance County, and he had absorbed the height of their traditions. Tommy and I played "Little Sod Shanty" and "Over the Waterfall"; we played "The Cuckoo" endlessly, loving its hard-rocking rhythm, striving to get my piano rolls and kicks and his five tight-strings to elide to a point of union—we had a lot of musical topspin together, and Tommy soon came to call my rhythmic playing "clawhammer piano."

He also often laughed and wondered why someone who loathed cold as much as I did now lived in such an ice chest as the cabin was, and why I had taken up the theater as a life pursuit, since both the small black boxes and the big barns of the theater world were always chilly.

Up in Austin's Quarter, a high cutover land nearby, just to the west, I collected firewood for both hearth and woodstove and kept things just as shanty-hot as I could.

Settled into this idyllic cabin home, at work on another musical, too (Hot Grog, a saga of the early 1700s Carolina pirates, with my Diamond Studs collaborator Jim Wann), rarely going to town, I found a new measure for those days: that of getting to know the Clover Garden wildlife quite closely and rather well.

Flying squirrels hit the 45-degree tin roof and slid down, and they loved the place so much they moved into an upstairs wall. The cabin owners wanted to get rid of them so badly that Eric Schopler hung a dozen or more huge foot-long rattraps on the upper outside wall—none of the traps ever caught a squirrel, but they clattered and rattled willy-nilly against that wall in the western wind, setting bizarre tempos, and they also gave the cabin the visual aspect of a macabre art installation, which I called, after that key floating domicile in Huckleberry Finn, the "House of Death."

Yet the cabin was nothing of the sort, except in one instance. For these squirrels were not alone in moving in.

One evening I put a Mose Allison record on the turntable (the jazz-blues pianist from Tippo, Mississippi, was one of my favorite performers, songwriters, and teachers) and sat down to listen closely to his Creek Bank. Before Mose had played a dozen measures of "Seventh Son," here came a bat swooping by at eye level. No amount of broom-swinging on my part could ground it, that night or the next three nights either, and one could not entertain guests like Tommy, nor keep one's "precarious grip on existence," as Conrad puts it, while a bat took to the air and came flying by close in on one's scalp and ears and eyes whenever it chose to.

So about the fourth night, when the bat flew around and up and landed and bunched itself up against the junction of ridge and roof beams, I took my best chance. My late father's bolt-action rifle at hand, I fired a single .22 short almost straight up and dropped it. Unpleasant, to be sure, yet necessary and effective.

Another night, something bumping about the kitchen woke me and bade me come down and check it out: when I threw on the light switch, I saw a possum, which had somehow pushed open the heavy but clearly unclosed kitchen door (mea culpa), standing before me, hissing.

Nothing to do but hiss back and approach cautiously—the possum retreated slowly, only, I think, due to my size, as my hissing was no louder than its was. As the animal backed out of the kitchen door, a sinister gleam in its eye advised me that it would return and that I should not believe for a second I had won this match.

One summer morning, I opened the cabin's heavy wooden front door and saw a cow standing over in the edge of the woods. The Schoplers at that time had no large livestock, so I telephoned timberman-farmer Clayton Rogers and his wife, Ruby, who lived about half a mile upstream on the other side of the creek.

Ruby Rogers answered, and I told her I had a cow just outside the cabin door.

"Well," she asked, "is it a black one or a big black-and-white spottedy one?"

"Spottedy," I replied, for the cow in question was a Holstein, our region's most popular, top-producing dairy breed.

"I'll call around," she said.

Before long, someone appeared in the drive, carrying a feed bag to lure the cow along, then sitting on the tailgate of a pickup truck that drove the feed-carrier slowly away as the hungry cow followed the truck, eating slowly from the bag as it did. I watched them from the cabin steps, a scarcely moving tableau slowly reaching the ridge road, truck and cow no more hurried than the cow alone might be, taking the thirty minutes or hour it would be to get back to the barn and milking parlor and go back into production, this morning's milking three hours done now, just not yet for this lost one, heavy with milk and still waiting—wanting—to be relieved of the four or five gallons she had made while she had strayed down to the cabin and stayed overnight.

In the kitchen another morning there, just as I was just about to set a coffeepot down, I noticed that the small four-burner stove had acquired, overnight, a fifth burner in its dead center.

A relatively small black snake had coiled itself in the middle of the stovetop on the white enamel in perfect mimicry of a dark electric coil. As the temperature in the cabin was cool, if not chilly, in all seasons, the snake made no movement, giving me just time enough to fetch an LP album cover (Bob Dylan's Isis) and the bottom of a rice steamer and slide the cover beneath the snake while clamping the steamer down on top of it, repatriating Mr. No-Shoulders to the rocks down by the creek.

In time I would get some coonhounds, and during their tenure the possums seemed to stay at bay, yet small furry beasts and all manner of reptiles constantly roamed the woods hereabouts, for this was their world, and all of them had served good and effective notice upon me that if I were going to keep living in the country, as the year or two I had first figured on being here soon went stretching out into four and five and more, the country was going to keep living with me.

And that, simply, was the way of it.

The Binghams

When I had first driven out to Bingham Township that late fall of 1975, I was a complete stranger to the township's southwestern corner, though I knew some of its middle territory miles away to the north.

Back in high school, in my 1948 four-cylinder Willys jeep, I had been traversing Dairyland Road from Calvander to Orange Grove (the capital of Bingham, as it were), passing the Grant Wood–style panorama, the rolling hills and fields of Maple View Farm on the way there, and then up Orange Grove Road and over to Chestnut Ridge, the camp where our youth group went fall and spring to learn about the Lord and His handiwork, paddling canoes and swimming in a big lake and staying in cabins and faux-Conestoga wagons, four bunks in each, for weekend stay-overs.

And I had heard of Hugh Wilson—the big six-foot-three pipe-smoking and beer-drinking dairyman and nephew of UNC Library's namesake Louis Round Wilson, always referred to in the old Chapel Hill Weekly as "the Squire of Bingham Township"—often. Hugh laughingly told me that he once held the Bank of Chapel Hill door downtown for my champion golfing aunt Estelle's mother, the altruistic, well-intentioned though imperious friend to the impoverished, Mrs. Robert Baker Lawson, and that she had turned to the Squire, astonished, saying, "Hugh Wilson, I'd've thought I'd drop my womb before the likes of you would ever hold a door for me."

I also once saw Hugh stand noisily in the Orange County Courthouse and tell the county commissioners, with hundreds in attendance, and the would-be Bingham Township airport developer (a choleric man named Hazzard) that he—Hugh—would hate to have to start using his shotgun, aimed upward, if aircraft from Hazzard's proposed (and much opposed) airfield started flying over his dairy farm and upsetting his sensitive cows, and, he added, "By God, I'll do it!" to deafening applause from the audience of Binghamites.

Bingham Township owed its name to a family of educators who operated academies both classical and military mostly though not exclusively in Orange County, North Carolina—one, early on, had begun in Wilmington, another, later, in Buncombe County. Yet there was a long spell when the Bingham School operated, from the mid-1840s to near the close of the Civil War, at Oaks, just north of Lloydtown out on NC 54 west of Chapel Hill and Carrboro. There, a contemporary "Inn at Bingham School" has welcomed guests for decades now and a historical marker about the school has long been a landmark halfway between our university town and Graham.

So when I drove west that first time to meet Eric Schopler and his wife, Miggie, about the log cabin they had for rent hard by Cane Creek, all I knew of Bingham Township then was the upper, Dairyland Road portion, all well north of Clover Garden.

And though the English department at UNC, where I had studied and would ere long come to teach, once had its headquarters in Bingham Hall, I certainly knew nothing more of those enterprising educators who had made well over a century's worth of family business under the name "Bingham School." Author Emily Bingham, who also studied in the building named to honor her great-great-grandfather Robert Hall Bingham, recently wrote of him, describing him as an ex-Confederate captain who had seen Lee's surrender at Appomattox and had come home to teach "Latin and white supremacy" at the Bingham School (by then in Mebane) by day and, in the 1870s, to go out riding in full regalia as a Ku Klux Klansman by night.

Nor did I know anything—yet—of the one who has for over a century been the best-known Bingham of them all: Robert Worth Bingham, son of Robert Hall Bingham, who grew up at Bingham School, who would invent the mysterious Order of Gimghoul with other classmates while at UNC–Chapel Hill in the late nineteenth century and have a brief fling with the sister of one of those comrades (Mary Lily Kenan from Kenansville). As a young attorney in Louisville, Kentucky, Emily Bingham also relates, he ran for commander in chief of the Sons of Confederate Veterans at a 1900 reunion, shook off being routed, and was a noted terpsichorean at that event's Lost Cause Ball.

A widower in 1913, he would revisit his affinity for Mary Lily, for, suddenly, with the death also in 1913 of oil-hotels-railroads-and-steamships tycoon Henry Flagler, the man who made Florida Florida, his widow Mary Lily Kenan Flagler became the wealthiest woman in the world.

Ah, the flame! Robert Bingham would very soon court and marry the widow Mary Lily, yet after less than a year of marriage he became the *widower* of Mary Lily Kenan Flagler Bingham, who mysteriously died in 1917 (rumorists wondered: Did Robert have her morphined to death in a Louisville bathtub? And was her body secretly exhumed in the dark of night from her Oakdale Cemetery grave in Wilmington with questionable authority by her kin so that drug tests of her tissue could be run?) and who left a $100 million fortune, bitterly fought over by Bingham and her Kenan blood kin.

A considerable amount of Mary Lily Kenan Flagler Bingham's money went by bequest to UNC–Chapel Hill, where it has long since supported the salaries and research funds of Kenan Distinguished Professors.

With Robert Bingham's share of inheritance, he bought two-thirds of the *Louisville Courier-Journal* and, not too many years later, used the paper and its influence fervently to champion Franklin Delano Roosevelt into the White House and then was rewarded as FDR's ambassador to the Court of St. James, London. Robert Worth Bingham may have learned enterprise in the family trade here in Bingham Township, yet he certainly refined and worked it to new heights, though not without severe controversy, in spots far larger than Oaks, North Carolina.

So I knew nothing, really, of the Binghams, or of Bingham School, on that late fall day in 1975, and I drove right on into Clover Garden, North Carolina, passing its invisible, gone-to-flinders 1800s ghost post office, knowing nothing of it, either, passing the old Morrow Mill on the road that bore its name without seeing at all the decommissioned mill or its mill pond, drove down the lane to Beechwood Farm, met the Schoplers, saw the cabin, and, before sunset, signed up to become a resident for the next twelve months in Clover Garden in Bingham Township, not knowing, either, that I would live here continuously for just shy of fifty years.

Hounds

Walking back home to the cabin from a woodland stroll one very cold winter night, I heard the choral howl of a pack of dogs.

There were wild dogs in Austin's Quarter, several square miles of rough woods and cutover lands that began not far beyond the cabin to the west. I kicked around in the dark and came up with a big stick. As I neared the cabin, I saw a dim light moving slowly in the woods not a hundred yards away. In more than four years, by now, living there by the creek, I had never seen anyone just wander by, day or night. I slipped into the cabin and then, through a downstairs window, watched the light disappear and reappear for a couple of minutes, the dogs barking and baying all the while.

There was not a shell or a cartridge in the house. We had shot them all up celebrating New Year's. I called Eric Schopler and told him some kind of a hunt was going on at the creek.

"You scared?" he said.

"Hell, yeah! I have no idea who this is!" By now I had seen a second light.

Eric came down in less than three minutes with a pistol and his border collie, Cubbie. Together we strode quickly into the woods and hailed the lights, though there was no reply.

"Hey, you there, hey!" we kept calling as we moved upstream along Cane Creek, and finally a man answered, "Yeah, hey!"

And then we all moved together, each party shining lights toward the other, and Eric Schopler and I learned what was up. What I should have realized.

"Coon hunting," one man said, walking up to us with a shotgun in the crook of his arm. "We been across the creek on Clayton Rogers's land, but a dog come over here and we got to get him back."

We spoke at ease then, and after a couple minutes three or four gigantic dogs (big as Lion in Faulkner's *Bear*) ran up among us and stopped, panting and pacing. They were huge hounds, eighty or ninety pounds apiece, and they towered over Eric's cowed and astounded border collie. Before I went back to the cabin, relieved and intrigued too, Eric and I watched the men and the dogs as they forded the creek and faded into the night, listening as the dark woods kept ringing with the songs of the baying hounds.

Four months later I went looking for the man who, I had learned from Clayton Rogers, had supplied the Cane Creek coon hunters with those giant dogs. Coming up NC 87 from Pittsboro, I pulled over and asked a man beside the road: "You know where Sherman Butler lives?"

"The hound dog man?"

"That's right."

"Well, what you do is, you go on up past the intersection there at Gum Springs, turn around, come back down and turn right at the intersection, then go on down all the way to a church, turn around, come back this way and take the first left."

A long straight dirt drive led to Sherman Butler's, and, as I came slowly toward his house, the lawn lifted up in a great groundswell of dogs—a hound swell—thirty or forty blueticks and almost as many redbones. They loped and snuffled about me as I headed for the back porch, where a stocky, ruddy-faced man in his late fifties stood with his hands in his pockets.

"Morning," he said.

"Morning. You Mr. Butler?"

"Yeah, I'm him." Sherman Butler had an easy manner, a gentle, almost muffled voice.

Just then an enormous bluetick dove through the flapping screen on the door, and in one fluid motion he was well over his head and shoulders down into a hundred-pound feed sack. We listened to him eat for a minute or two, his crunching jaws sounding like a small rockcrusher.

A car drove up and a small man wearing a baseball cap emerged and strode familiarly over to the porch. We spoke all around, and then the new man, a comrade of Butler's named Solomon Holt, nodded at the feeding dog.

"He's really putting it on, ain't he, Sherman?"

"Yeah, well, he's a big boy, Sol—he's hungry."

I told Sherman Butler I wanted a bluetick pup, and he said he had none just then. The three of us walked about the yard while Sherman and Sol tried for a while to sell me on any number of the young dogs that were around.

"That dog's got a good mouth," Sol would say. "I like a dog with a good mouth, don't you, Sherman?"

And Sherman would nod and I would nod but say nothing about buying him, and Sol would regard another dog and say, "Now that one's got a good nose, be a good coon dog, won't he, Sherman?" or "Look at the ears on that one, you can tell a lot about a dog from his ears."

There were deep, hoarse cries from a large bluetick chained to a fuel-tank doghouse in the side yard. "That's Joe," Sherman Butler said. "I'm going to be breeding one of my bigger bitches to old Joe there—probably get some big dogs out of that litter, like you looking for. It's that Vaughn breeding out of Arkansas. You call me in about six weeks or so."

Later that summer, my friend Jake Mills and I drove down to Gum Springs to see the new litter. We each knelt in turn to duck into an antique henhouse where an old gyp, not the mother, was nursing the small snub-nosed bluetick pups.

I held several of the males, my hand under their bellies, till I found the one that seemed neither too slack nor too wild. In another couple weeks, when he was big enough, I came back and got him for good.

He was all gunmetal blue ticking, with a big black saddleback patch of color, and he had doubled in size since I picked him out. I took him home and named him: Blue Tom Cotton.

To the manner (and manor) born, I thought, when the first thing he did was run up under the cabin porch and lie there listlessly, looking worthless.

Cotton was baying in no time at all and taking delight in it, and he ate steadily in all weathers through the seasons. His Arkansan stock, which Sherman Butler brought into this part of the country, had been bred up in size to make bear dogs for the Upper Peninsula hunters of Michigan.

He weighed a hundred pounds by his first birthday, and on Thanksgiving morning of his second year he devoured an entire twenty-two-inch apple tart, intended for a community dinner, in barely half a minute.

As he grew into a giant, he became famous around the Clover Garden neighborhood—both for his size and for his hoarse roaring howl. Down at Jerry Copeland's corner grill they called him "Old Rattler," after the famous-long-ago Grandpa Jones song, and my timberman neighbor Clayton Rogers once told me, "It may be a half a mile or more from my house to your cabin, but when that big blue dog really gets going, I swear I look over and he's rattling the window lights." Sherman Butler gave me some copies of coonhound magazines he had lying around, *American Cooner* and *Full Cry*, full of ads for vaunted studs that could chop-mouth, howl and tree, and stand and serve, and he told me I ought to take Cotton down to the big Fourth of July coon dog congress outside of Candor. This annual shindig of hounds always drew several hundred people and about as many coon dogs, and it was a long, hot Fourth of July day of baroo-ing and chop-mouth barking from these legions of bluetick, black and tans, Treeing Walkers, redbones, redtick, English, and even brindled Plott hounds from the high Carolina hills, this last breed soon voted by the General Assembly to be the state dog of North Carolina.

This was the biggest crowd Blue Tom Cotton had ever seen, and he did not put on that good of a show. He failed to really open up much at the raccoon

Hounds in water race, Candor, North Carolina, early 1980s

in the cage up the tree, and when it came time for a race across a lake against other hounds, Cotton refused to go anywhere near the water. Nearly a dozen people came up to me after this dog-world humiliation, offering sympathy in earnest.

"Oh, I can tell he's a good dog, he's gon' finish out great," they would say, "but he ain't done much of this, has he?"

"No," I answered. "This is his first time out."

"Well, that's the thing," someone else said. "You got to *work* with 'em."

Working with him, as best I could tell, would have involved going out in a boat on a pond thirty or forty-five minutes at a time, several times a week, and luring him into the water by waving an old coonskin at him. Then he would be ready for next summer's events. I simply decided to neglect this part of Cotton's education, and I reported this, and his poor showing, to Sherman Butler sometime later when I was boarding the hound with him.

"Oh, they pick it up on their own," Mr. Butler said. "That's just for fun, that big get-together and all. I wouldn't worry about it."

Then we went on out to the old dairy barn where Cotton and my other dog, by comparison a slight—only seventy pounds—black-and-tan named Posey, were tethered. It was summer twilight, and Sherman Butler told me how they'd fared: "Now, that black dog of yours, she went to eating first time I fed her, but the blue dog, he was so lonely for you he cried the first three or four days till it looked to rain and I moved him from off that chain tied on the oak tree and carried him down to the barn where I had your black dog. After that they were both pretty good and ate all right too.

"In a month or so we'll catch up and take a dog or two apiece and go see can't we catch the old coon once he starts moving about. Not on a real cold day—I don't like the cold and can't go as hard and long as I could when I was your age, but later on in October, November, come on and we'll go out."

This was the last time I would see Sherman Butler—he died on Christmas Eve that year. I never heard what became of all those dogs, but I will never forget the way, whenever he walked about his grounds, from six to ten dogs would lazily rise and move along with him apace, not as if expecting food or even a petting, just wanting to be close to the hound-dog man of Gum Springs.

Cotton throve.

The great blue dog spent his days ripping at rotten trees, setting up echoing bellows from the hollows near the cabin. Anytime I took him somewhere, he drew comments. I had him in my pickup once at Lewis Allen's store out on NC 54.

"You gon' hunt coons with that dog, I reckon?" Mr. Allen said.

I thought better of telling him the dog was a porch sitter and an intended house pet.

"Squirrels," I said.

"Squirrels!?" Mr. Allen laughed big and loud. "Why, he'd scare everything for two miles around out of the woods, first time he opened up. You ain't gon' get no squirrels with that dog!"

I was out walking along the west end of Morrow Mill Road one morning, and Cotton went running into the yard where the very genial Jazz Thompson, an African American neighbor and friend, was sitting in a kitchen chair with a magazine on his lap. Jazz said, laughing: "Whoa! Out the way, here comes old King Pin!"

I called the dog and when he wouldn't come went to fetch him.

The magazine was a catalog, and Jazz was puzzling over the way the confusing information was laid out. He wanted to order by phone the right size sausage plate for his grinder from this discount mail-order house, but he seemed ready for a break, and we talked for a little while.

Jazz was an active man, a man of parts: he farmed, he did repairs, he knew his way around a still. He laughed in a heartbeat, especially when he was telling me what the judge had said when he sent Jazz home from court one day: "Now, Mr. Thompson, I don't want to hear any more about you and white liquor." "Yes, sir, your honor," Jazz said he told the judge, adding for me: "I made me a copper worm and I was set up back on the creek with a still before that month was done, I sure was!"

Then Jazz returned his attention to Cotton, exclaiming, "If I was twenty years younger, I'd be out in the woods four, five nights a week with that hound."

"I'd hate to see his ears get all torn up," I said.

"Aw, no," said Jazz, "that'd just make him *right*. Make him better looking and worth more too. Yeah. Old King Pin."

Another time out walking, Cotton and I were suddenly being stalked by an old low-riding white Chevrolet. A thin teenage boy was behind the wheel, and the man in the passenger seat, a middle-aged character with dark, greased-down hair, was sipping a Blue Ribbon and staring at the hound.

"How much that dog weigh?" the man said.

"About a hundred pounds."

"It don't look like he misses many meals."

"No," I said. "He eats by the clock."

The Chevrolet engine went *hudnhudnhudn* as they drove along slowly, matching our walking pace.

"I got a chihuahua," the man said, "'bout the size'd fit in a teacup. You want to trade that blue dog for him?"

"How much does he weigh?"

"Two and a half, three pounds."

"Well," I said, "sounds like you'd get about ninety-seven pounds more dog out of this trade than I would."

"Yeah," he said, nestling the Blue Ribbon in his lap as he head-pointed at Cotton, "but then you ain't got to feed him no more."

One afternoon we were out in the hayfields, Eric Schopler and his sons Bobby and Tommy, his stepson Oliver, and me, the bunch of us getting up 500 or 600 bales before the rain. Edgar Pickard bellowed like a drover as he piloted his train of farm vehicles, a tractor, a baler, and a hay wagon behind that, down the raked hay lanes. At one point the grizzle-bearded dairy-man turned the tractor much too sharply and promptly broke the tongue of the hay wagon. Eric and his stepson went off to fetch another wagon, and Edgar, streaming with sweat and happy for the break, talked dogs with me.

"William Morrow tells me you got some treeing dogs."

"That's right."

"What'll they tree? William says he's seen your bluetick tree a squirrel. You gon' breed him?"

"Might," I said.

"Well," Edgar said, "I'd like to have me a pup to go possum hunting with, if they ain't asking too much for 'em. I don't have that kind of money. I ain't gon' pay no *war prices* now!"

I thought Cotton had plenty of running room in the woods and ridges, but just shy of half a mile to the north above the deep woods was NC Highway 54. One night, an old woman with a quavering voice telephoned and said: "Your dog is dead down at Lewis Allen's store and Lewis has got his collar." Over to Lewis Allen's I went, and the flinty Mr. Allen said: "He's down yonder in that concrete ditch. Whole pack of 'em was chasing a deer, ran out in front of a woman driving a Toyota, tore the front of that thing all up."

"And you have the collar?"

"In the back of my truck out there."

I got the collar, then went back into the store to thank Mr. Allen again for getting it and for having his wife call me. But Allen, for whom a call to me at that time would have been long distance, costing twenty-five cents, let me know that what he'd really done was wait for someone on my exchange to happen by and had given her the assignment: "I didn't call you," he said, almost with a snarl. "You're on the *Mebane* line." For the great blue dog I made a cairn down a ravine in the woods at home. In the years since, I have often thought of his huge full-throated howl, his vigorous ear-flapping, his table-clearing tail, the long, high lonesome *ahooooo* he made sometimes. I have not missed his cross-country jaunts or the subsequent phone calls from people eight or ten miles away across the Haw River—"Come get your dog!"—including one older woman whose telephone call is seared into my memory: "Is this Simpson?" she had asked, and I said yes. "You got a great big blue dog?" Yes ma'am, I said. "Well, I got him tied to the back-porch stair rail at my house over at Eli Whitney—you come get him right now 'cause I ain't gonna *feed him!*"

Just before Christmas one year I saw Ricky Worley down at Jerry Copeland's corner grill, that is to say the commercial district of Clover Garden, both of us waiting on barbeque sandwiches. Ricky was a dairyman who lived and worked nearby, up toward Orange Grove, then in his early thirties, a tall, thin fellow with a mustache and an "I Hunt Blueticks" ballcap. Years before he had sought me out, wanting Blue Tom Cotton for stud. For Cotton's service he offered me the pick of the litter, but the arrangement we actually worked out was that he would board Cotton in his pens from time to time.

"I got a nice bunch of pups now," he said at the grill, describing them and comparing them to Cotton or to Cotton's pup that was most like him. He counted them up, and when he got to six, Ricky shook his head and said, "You know what it costs to feed that bunch of hounds!?"

As I got into my car, he invited me to come around and take a look at what he had. He also let me know he was of a mind to give away a dog or two, and for a few moments I thought only of the sheer wonder of the great blue dog, forgetting all the vexations of living with livestock, forgetting that everyone had told me, "You can't make a pet out of a coonhound" and that everyone had been right. Ricky knew I had his number, and I know he could see the desire in my eyes when he leaned toward my rolled-down car window and said, grinning, "Yeah, you just give me a call when you're ready to get back in the bluetick business."

Yet I never was quite ready again, so I never did make that call.

Owl

One Saturday a little before midnight, I drove home from town and swerved on the Cane Creek bridge to avoid a clump, a dark jacket it looked like, in my lane right in the middle of the bridge. As I passed it I got a quick glimpse of what it really was: a very large bird.

A great horned owl.

I stopped the car, backed up, and parked, leaving my headlights on and beaming them across the bridge.

The owl lay stock-still, and after regarding it for a few moments, I curled an index finger into each set of talons and lifted it from the roadway. Upside down, its wings fell away from its body and spread wide open. No damage was apparent, till I saw that one of the owl's two feathered horns was missing, and I reckoned that it must have flown just a tad too low and clipped either a passing car or the top rail of the bridge. A concussion that cost it its life and one horn but left its body intact.

Carefully, I put the owl into the wayback of the station wagon, drove the last mile home to the cabin on Cane Creek, and then wrapped the owl up in a plastic bag and put it into the freezer.

It was an absolutely beautiful bird, and I would get it stuffed and mounted.

Or so I thought.

When we spoke on the phone a day or two later, the Sanford taxidermist asked me where I had found the owl.

"On the road near where I live," I said. "And it's in almost perfect shape."

"That may be," he said. "Any shot in it?"

"I don't think so," I replied, telling him my theory that the big raptor must have clipped the bridge rail or grazed a passing car.

"But you don't know for sure," the taxidermist said.

"No."

"Are you connected with a museum or a school?" he asked.

"No." This was several years before I began teaching writing at UNC.

"Well, buddy, my advice to you is get that owl out of your house and bury it or just throw it in the creek."

"What? But it's such a great specimen!"

"That may be," he said again. "But you're not supposed to be in possession of it—that's a federally protected bird, and right now you're sitting on a $500 fine. Best get rid of it."

We rang off, and I told Eric Schopler about this, showing him the bird in the bag in the freezer.

"Well, I'm connected with a school," he enthused. "I could get it stuffed."

And that is just what happened. Eric took the frozen owl down to the taxidermist in Lee County, who immediately X-rayed it to determine if there was any shot in its body and, finding none, agreed to stuff and mount it for Eric,

Simpson's Owl

who would keep it at his internationally renowned autistic children's program office at UNC–Chapel Hill.

When this trophy came back from the shop, Eric decided to hang it at home, high above the Joanna Hole on Cane Creek, and just admire it for a little while before taking it to his office on campus. He invited me at once to come up and join him.

The great horned owl sat high above his dining room table. Perched, I should say, to make it appear to be on alert and ready to lift off a branch in flight after prey. Quite a sight, and upon the plaque to which this natural action figure was now affixed, a small bright plate's legend read:

Simpson's Owl, Cane Creek Valley, North Carolina

Of course this was gratifying, not only to receive some sort of credit for the find and the save but also to have one's name paired with such a magnificent creature.

Months later, long after Eric had placed Simpson's Owl on his office wall on the Chapel Hill campus, he told me over sour mash one evening that I had really gotten a whole lot more out of that owl than I might have imagined.

"What do you mean?" I asked.

"Every visitor who walks into my office," he said (he who had visitors from all over the world, from Sweden to Japan, all of them hoping to learn from and make use of his and TEACCH's revolutionary analytical and testing practices concerning autism), "looks right past me at the owl and virtually *demands* to hear the story of Simpson's Owl before we can talk about anything else. I mean *every single visitor!*"

"What do you do?"

"I tell them the story," Eric said. "The whole story. And they *always* have a lot of questions. I tell the tale of you and that owl all the time. I'm surprised your ears haven't burnt off yet!"

Auction

When I first moved to Clover Garden, there was little horse-riding culture, whereas nowadays there are plenty of boarding and riding spots, *dressage* even, here and there around Bingham Township.

In those older times, timberman Clayton Rogers's son had a brown horse in the Cane Creek–side field behind his place, and that horse always seemed to be peering out from a rise behind that field, just his head, down at the road and the bridge over the creek itself—*the horse that looks over the hill,* I called him.

Yet the real eye-catcher at the Rogers farm to me was Charlie, a big-chested and much darker horse that was in a field of his own in front of Clayton and his wife Ruby's home, reflecting their sense of how special he was. For Ol' Charlie, as they always called him, had done a lifetime's worth of work, snaking logs off hillsides and ridges and tight turns along creek banks and bringing them to the log truck that would take them away to a mill. And when he was beginning to have a harder time and showing signs of the toll of all that work, Clayton and his brother Pete simply let Charlie retire, let him just stay home here in Clover Garden and take it easy for the rest of his days. No way in hell would they have thought for a second of sending him to the auction house down in Siler City, thirty-five miles and a whole different world away.

One night back in the 1970s, we three great comrades—writer Loyd Little, dairyman and builder Bruce Miles, and I—had gone together to that small livestock auction down in Siler City. Loyd was well into equines and even kept a mule named George Washington but called Wash in a paddock across from his Frog Level home northeast of Orange Grove (a live mule, mind, not a dead mule like you hear so much about, given Jake Mills's "Equine Gothic" objective litmus test of what was and was not southern fiction—a dead mule in a literary work meant it qualified; no dead mule, close but no cheroot).

We walked slowly through the Chatham County stockyard as if we were buyers and heard talk both knowledgeable and outlandish from other men looking over the animals.

Once in the small arena we sat high above the ring, watching unsteady, spavined horses with uncertain footing being led in by their handlers, shown for short stints, sold in blisteringly fast auctioneering, and then led off. One horse was so far gone it would have fallen down had it not leaned on the wooden wall of the ring. Not one animal seemed appealing or healthy enough for any of us to consider making a bid. These were horses quite literally on their last legs.

We had come hoping to see quarter horses, Appaloosas, paints, maybe even a majestic draft horse, a Norman or a Percheron or two, but we were sadly mistaken. In the noble world of the horse, little good was showing that night at the Siler City stockyard—little but ill care, age, overwork, and owners who had turned away from their equine charges in their final hours of need.

The buyers there were agents of dog-food companies who would take the old horses away before midnight to their last end.

One brief, malicious exchange we could not help but overhear, out in the stables when we were on the way in, seemed to have set the tone of the evening, and sharply so.

"How old is he?" one fellow had said, pointing at a wobbly horse in its stall.

"The book's in his mouth," a passing stranger said nastily. "*Read it!*"

After a scant hour in that doleful arena, we three got up and left, driving dispiritedly through the Chatham darkness, not saying much at all, on up through the small agrarian crossroads of Silk Hope, Snow Camp, Eli Whitney, on toward home, toward Clover Garden, where Ol' Charlie enjoyed a far, far better fate than any of the horses whose last sad motions we had just witnessed that night.

Gentle Giants

Outside the horse barn in Raleigh, under the Hunter's Moon, were the ruckus and lights of the state's great fall fair—and a whole world away from that dismal auction in Chatham County. Inside, before a crowd of hundreds in absolute hush, twenty-seven teams of draft horses strained to pull twice their weight and more in silvery lead ingots loaded onto big wooden sleds. Having joined the North Carolina Draft Horse and Mule Association soon after our Siler City excursion, I now wanted to see the biggest, healthiest horses and what all they could do.

At three-quarters to a full ton each, these gentle giants were only yesterday the greatest force in American agriculture. Then, as the tractor took everything about horsepower but the horse itself, they were abandoned or slaughtered, and the nation's herd was nearly gone by 1960.

Were it not for the constant, colorful display of the Anheuser-Busch Clydesdales, the draft horse would by now have the same mystique in the public mind as the unicorn. But the heavy horses never went out of style with the Amish, nor with a handful of other midwestern breeders; and, since the low point, more and more small farmers and loggers, as well as big-hitch enthusiasts, have joined the postwar holdouts and brought back the numbers of one of mankind's best and noblest friends.

Still, the first question many asked as they stared upon these beasts in unimaginative awe was: "What do you *do* with a horse like that?"

In the late afternoon before the pulling contest had started, owners congregated outside the arena.

Boys sat by stall doors, where the air was thick with smells of horse and hay and new wood. The men and women who brought the heavy horses kicked the dirt with the pointed toes of design-stitched cowboy boots and stood talking beside their red and deep-blue and silver-gray pickups and long gooseneck trailers. Roy Cash and James Jenkins, from Lonely Oak Farm north of Lynchburg, talked about whether or not to buy a $5,600 trailer as they waited for pulling time. Their team of big Belgians, Bert and Dick, had worked as many as twenty acres in a season at Lonely Oak, hay raking, harrowing, and skidding logs.

"They go places tractors can't go," said Cash as he laid an easy hand on Bert, a 2,000-pound strawberry roan with hooves the size of a man's head.

"His weight's off a little," Cash said. "Bert's been up as high as twenty-two fifty."

A hundred yards away, a Warrenton woman in a black cowboy hat nuzzled up to Babe and Dolly, her dapple-gray draft mules—sired by the same mammoth jack stud but born out of two sister Percheron mares. "We work two, three acres of corn and beans with them," said Harriet Cooper of Double-C Farms. "As a team or singly, they work good either way."

The sun set lower in the floury clouds and the wind went through the sweet gums and big pines in breezes and light gusts. As the October evening drew on, a throaty steam whistle blew over the lake and up the hill toward the agricultural relics exhibit. Beyond that was the dull thudding of midway rock music and the collective roar of a crowd pulled to the apex of a loop-de-loop.

Men hitched and harnessed their draft horse teams and warmed them up, driving slowly round a dusty ring near the stalls. Then the twenty-seven teams queued up and entered the arena, drivers prepared to meld wills with their beasts and show just what they could and did do with horses like that: Good hard work.

Onto the sawdust floor they came, all but encircling the scraped red-clay sled lane at the center like a great horseshoe of horses.

A number of the teams were from North Carolina, which by the 1980s had led the South in rebuilding America's population of heavy horses. But many were far from home: teams from Virginia, Ohio, Maine, Michigan, and Maryland had come a long way to pull a lot of weight.

Here were the two work-stock breeds much favored over the far better-known Scottish Clydesdales: sorrel, barrel-chested Belgians and massive black and dapple-gray Percherons, the French breed that a millennium ago carried armored soldiers and went armored themselves into battle (and which some Carolinians refer to casually as *Persians*).

Each team in turn moved up to the sled of lead weights with one driver holding a long dark pair of reins and two others carrying the hitch bar that they would drop and hook onto the sled. At the clanking of the chains as hitches fell and caught, the horses jerked tight and forward at the drivers' commands, some scarcely audible, some a sharp steady "Git! Git! Git!" that filled the hall.

Time and again, the teams showed their mettle, their single-minded and strong-hearted desire to please mankind by doing its heaviest work. And the crowd that had shunned the noisy, tawdry midway for the evening pulled with them, in spirit and in silence, for any outburst during a pull could make a team think its job was done before it really was.

When the judge whistled that the team had pulled its requisite twenty-seven feet, the crowd cheered and gave voice to its delight in the strength and beauty of the biggest horses in the land.

The weights on the sled had started at 4,000 pounds, and all teams pulled through. Then a white truck with hydraulic pincers lifted more ingots on and

Lester Ray plowing with three-Percheron hitch, between Clover Garden and White Cross, November 2023

Three Percherons

increased the sled weight to 5,000 for a round, to 5,500 for another, and then to 6,000 pounds for a fourth.

An announcer over loudspeakers said, "Whoever has the Silverado outside with mules tied to it, your mules have chewed themselves loose!"

All the teams were still in competition after 6,000 pounds. There was a steady *hoosh* from the horse barn's enormous fans and the winding sound of the hydraulic pincer arm on the weights truck that had moved up the lane with another 500 pounds.

It was between 9 and 10 p.m. when the truck was adding the lead that would be too much for some teams.

The state's commissioner of agriculture entered the barn with a television crew in tow. He moved along aisles and down stairs, grinning and nodding and shaking hands. Atop his head was a small silver-gray Stetson with crimped crown, and he had a long cigar that he now clenched between his teeth and now waved like a baton.

The commissioner made his way to the ring to pose with the horses, and this was the picture: fifty-four of these living, breathing partners, symbol of the small farmer, dwarfing the big man (the *Sodfather*, so called) during whose nineteen-year tenure the state had lost half its farms.

Drivers moved their teams up for the next round, and at 6,500 pounds some started to drop out. Through three more rounds this went, up through three and a half, three and three-quarters, and, finally, four tons of lead.

Twenty-seven teams pulled hard and well, and not simply at the sled. These mighty creatures had pulled at the hearts of hundreds, most of whom were seeing draft horses and mules for the first time, and some of whom were seeing them once again, yet only after a very long time.

The horses took grand powerful steps, and the drivers' booted feet skidded on the sawdust as their teams trotted to the sled. In the end it was a North Carolina–Virginia team, Duke and King, that got the most out of straining heart and muscle, shoulder, flank and leg. They pulled as hard as any breath-drawing creature can, as if the earth would not turn on its axis unless a four-ton sled moved to glory down a red-clay lane in Raleigh.

Broke Spoke

Frank Queen and I had been to the Cat's Cradle in town one Saturday night to hear our favorite country rock band, Bro T Holla, and after they had all but closed down the great old bistro, we drifted on homeward about

1:30 in the morning. At the western edge of Carrboro, a thin boy, thirteen at most, had his thumb out, and, surprised to see such a youth abroad at that late hour, we stopped and picked him up.

"Where you heading?" I said from the shotgun seat. Frank was behind the wheel of his gold-colored Buick ("You always want to have a car that's the color of some form of currency," he used to say).

"Broke Spoke," the boy said laconically and offered no more.

The small, low-slung roadhouse on our way home sat just east of White Cross, well town-ward of Clover Garden, and had had a number of names over the years—Paul's Place when it was a prime neighborhood steakhouse, the Little Bar when it featured televised sports and fuel-tank-cooker pork-scorching, and in times yet to come the diminutive yet lively music hall would be called the Kraken.

Just then, though, the place was a biker bar that on weekend nights would have dozens of Harley choppers parked and listing left as if they had all been racked there just so. A motorcycle wheel with one missing spoke hung upon a sign, and that was all the name and advertisement it needed, causing this non-rider to recall the insider exchange Hunter Thompson once heard between a reporter and the hard-driving chief of the Hell's Angels, Sonny Barger:

"How do you choose your members?" the reporter had asked.

"We don't choose 'em," said Barger the chief. "We *recognize* 'em."

Six miles lay between where we picked the boy up and where we would let him off, and he never said a word along the way. As we neared the spot, Frank and I remembered that the icebox was bare back at the cabin and knew if we wanted a Sunday afternoon cold one the next day, a takeout would be in order.

"Up there," the kid spoke at last, and Frank pulled off to the right and came to a stop. As the kid was opening the back-right door and getting out, I said I would go in and get us a little something for tomorrow. Quickly, before I had even pulled my door handle, the kid leaned into my open window (it was summertime, still nearly eighty degrees past midnight) and said with the thin, reedy, and harsh voice of an old man, and with a tone full of both warning and threat: "There ain't *nothin'* for you in there, mister."

"M. B.," said Frank to me at once, "we're leaving."

And as Frank eased away, the boy clambered down the short bank to the parking lot, threading himself through the collection of dozens of high-powered wheels, and disappeared into the Broke Spoke tavern, packed with riders and ablaze with lights and, according to this strange, world-weary boy, welcoming only those that its tribe could recognize.

Merritt's

Former fishmonger Dick Gibbs installed a Swedish smoker in one of the two bays in Merritt's classic white-stucco-walled, red-terra-cotta-roofed Esso station on the south side of Chapel Hill and began offering hot barbeque sandwiches in the 1929 vintage spot, a town-meets-country epicenter that for fifty years had never offered its customers anything warmer than pinto beans or sardines in a can. Then, a few years later, Robin and Bob Britt turned the corner when they started slinging single- and double-BLTs at the public and created a roaring land-office grill business that has run hard for thirty years and has shown no signs of abating. Journalist and comrade David Zucchino of the New York Times (a two-time Pulitzer winner for his trenchant coverage both foreign and domestic) and I have contributed to the roar and the crush, and we have witnessed many a time when Merritt's has become so crowded at lunchtime, such a tight spot that folks can hardly draw a breath.

Eben Merritt, who ran a gravel-hauling business before he filled in enough of the hillside framed by South Columbia Street and Purefoy Street to put his small Esso gas station there, unloaded boxcars of lime for my grandfather Page when the spur line brought the train to the center of campus and when he was directing the university's building boom of the 1920s. "I never knew a man who would chase a nickel so far," Granddaddy (who nonetheless respected Merritt's endless work ethic) once told me.

Author and UNC writing professor Phillips Russell called Merritt "the president of south Chapel Hill," adding, "He'll talk coon hunting with the best of them. And if you want to discuss your troubles, he'll talk about them too."

Once, back in the autumn of 1951, Eben Merritt and three younger Black men who were hunting together one night in the foggy New Hope Creek lowlands east of Chapel Hill got two raccoons by one in the morning. A journalist along for the hunt wrote that after the men had left the woods, Merritt's "truck lights fell on a possum at the side of the road. He stopped, caught it by the tail, put it in the sack with the raccoons and continued on to town. For those who hadn't been on a coon hunt before, it was an exciting event. For Eben Merritt any coon hunt is, and the one to come is the most exciting of all."

My father used to drop down from the Page family's home just up South Columbia a hundred yards, where my father and mother were courting in the early days of World War II, and talk dogs (Merritt let some of his coon dogs—he kept blueticks, black and tans, and redbones, with names like Ole Red, Blackie, and Rattler—lay about in the store) with Merritt, who by then had just enough age and authority to be referred to as "the Cap'n" and addressed, by one and all entering the station, as "Cap'n."

Cap'n Merritt was thought to be both notoriously miserly (he kept anywhere from a few hundred to a few thousand dollars in cash rolled up in the big pocket of his overalls and at least once paid $25,000 in cash for a dump truck to a heavy equipment dealer who had thought Merritt was only a poor country bumpkin wandering into the showroom just to gaze at the big shiny machines) and famously generous (he kept many a family, without regard to race, fed and in their homes with well-timed loans when they were in need, and, further, he kept up with who owed him what and did not worry over it much).

After standing silently near his plate-glass window where he let big bunches of bananas bake till they were near black from the late-afternoon sun ("I like 'em ripe"), saying nothing except thank you to customers and just listening to the men who gathered daily around the benches and the space heater and told tales of the logwoods, of cattle, of hogs, fishing, and hunting, mostly, though never of women, sometimes Cap'n Merritt would suddenly, surprisingly, open up at full volume (he had a thin, raspy voice) with a tale in which he was either the hero or the figure of fun, to wit:

Merritt and another man had gone turkey hunting on a cutover tract of timberland down in Chatham County, which he had bought almost sight unseen—he knew where it was; had seen it from the road; knew who had owned it, what had been growing on it, and how much timber had come off it (likely at the hands, saws, and trucks of his cousin Glynn Fields, a large affable timberman with black horn-rimmed glasses, a regular at the station); and the price was right. So the venture after turkeys was the Cap'n's first time actually walking *on* his new land. No luck hunting this particular day, so Cap'n Merritt suggested that the two of them roam down and find and meet the man, an African American, who had long been a tenant there and establish relations between them.

When they walked into the clearing where the man's cabin stood, he leapt alarmed from the rock step at his cabin door and approached them, feeling Lord only knows what level of real fear and fright at the sight of two white men he had never seen before, each armed with a 12-gauge shotgun. Before Cap'n Merritt could introduce himself and his companion, the tenant vigorously warned them away: "You gentlemen, you got to get away from here— fine with me you hunt all you want, but I don't own these woods, just rent here a long time, and this land's got a new owner—Cap'n Eben Merritt, has the fillin' station, and I ain't met him yet, but from what everybody tells me, he is one *quare son of a bitch!*"

Though the old tenant had never laid eyes on Merritt before, he had heard enough and had captured the Cap'n's peculiar nature in a phrase. And Cap'n Merritt took no issue with it at all, often telling that story on himself, laughing at its last line till he was weak and wheezing, even knowing his listeners had all heard it many times before. Another of his oft-repeated tales was that of the evening a man came in to rob the store (everyone near and far knew about the smoking wad of money in the top pocket of his overalls) and Merritt swiftly got his shotgun but the robber grabbed the barrel, wrestling Merritt partway down the stairs to the basement in back, disarming him and snatching the cash in almost the same motion. Young college women accustomed to filling up their cars at the station, having heard of this fracas, started to drop by in droves to commiserate with the Cap'n, which always involved tight sympathetic hugs from the women. The loafers observed that all this outpouring of empathy and affection Merritt received seemed to assuage him a good deal over the loss of $700 or $800 and that for what he got, the robbery might have been well worth it and then some.

Where in more recent times a collection of covered picnic benches sat out back, there once grew a chinaberry tree, and there in the 1970s and 1980s gathered a small group of men who disdained the benches and the beer-drinking indoors and had their own informal bar of harder stuff beneath that tree. Every now and again, one of them would enter the store to obtain some sodas, mixers for what they had out back. Cap'n Merritt of course knew exactly what they were up to, gave tacit permission and sold them the drinks, and always laughed as the man headed out, saying, "They're having another meeting of the Chanty-berry Crew!"

Inside, though, the musings were modest and generally well-mannered (though to the bathroom door *was* tacked a white license plate with red and blue lettering as the legend to a drawing of a pipe that went from this bathroom to the US Capitol, saying, "Flush twice—it's a long way to Washington!"), and the groups always included several doctors down from Memorial Hospital just up the hill; artist-professor John Allcott and his gorgeous Weimaraner Maxine (whom he had taught to sit still with a Cheez Doodle upon her snout until Dr. Allcott said "Okay!" and she would then flip it up into the air and catch it: a most popular trick of an afternoon); and cousin Glynn Fields in from the logwoods.

I recall Glynn laughing lustily along with all the rest when the Cuckleberry Jones story got told, and in fact it may have been Glynn who told it: Seems

Cuckleberry Jones, a state wildlife officer, was having a devil of a time catching these two men who, Jones just knew, having found some of their pond-side dead fish as evidence, were shocking and stunning fish with electricity in a certain Chatham County pond, using the wire leads of an old hand-crank telephone run down into the water off the side of their jonboat and then hauling in the stunned bream and catfish, tossing the smaller ones that they did not want to fool with off onto the bank, tipping Cuckleberry Jones to them and what they were about.

Yet he had never managed to catch them in the act, so at last he put out word, which he knew would easily reach this pair, that he was going on vacation, up to the mountains of western Carolina, for two or maybe even three weeks. He gave this ruse a week or so to take effect, and the two men, as he suspected, were having a field day with their telephone and the fish.

So on one morning, well into his supposed vacation, he went out early to the pond in question, hid himself in the bankside woods, and waited.

Before long, here they came, along with their hand-crank phone and a whopper of a cooler for their catch of the day. And to hold their beer.

They pushed off in the jonboat and got to fishing. And to drinking. And pretty soon they were laughing and laughing, and whichever one was cranking the phone would say, "Calling Cuckleberry Jones!" and laugh maniacally.

And then they would settle down, gather the stunned fish, and trade off working the phone.

"Calling Cuckleberry Jones!"

Two grown men, Wildlife Resources criminals in fact, rolling around with an old crank telephone in a jonboat, about to fall out of it laughing themselves silly: "Calling Cuckleberry Jones!"

Till from the woods at that last call emerged Officer Jones, the man himself, holding his badge in one hand and his drawn revolver in the other, grinning at the two and saying slowly, "Hel-LO!"

And there was great big Marvin Bennett in from plowing up garden plots for town folks on his 8N Ford tractor with its gray elephant-eared fenders, which he would drive to the station from his ridgetop home (and his tractor shed with white liquor in milk jugs stashed away in the hay) across Morgan Creek a mile and a half away; Pizza Johnny from one of the takeout places, who would often bring us surprise pizzas, which customers had called in for but never picked up, and set them up on the rich-brown space heater to stay warm while we all indulged; and writer-professor Phillips Russell, who would walk down from his Chase Avenue home just up the hill. Phillips said very little at Merritt's, though I do recall how he once raised the courtroom roof during a town hall hearing over whether or not to allow an apartment complex to be built tightly adjacent to Chase Avenue, Phillips rising and noisily grasping the long bench in front of him and exhorting the board: "I thought we had more *friendliness* in this town, I thought we had more *neighborliness* in this town, I thought we had more good *common sense* in this town—but it turns out all we've got is *blind mercantilism stalking the streets!*" To great applause, he fell back onto his bench and sighed.

I first took note of Merritt's on Christmas Day 1964, when my mother proposed sending me forth to buy a loaf of bread for hot turkey sandwiches.

"Nothing'll be open," I said.

"Oh, yes, there will—Merritt's will be open; he never closes for *anything!*"

And to my astonishment, she was right.

Years later, Cap'n Merritt (now well used to Jake Mills and my stopping by sometimes in the late afternoon) allowed me to borrow and use a garage bay when it might be empty, and Jim Wann and I changed out mufflers and starters on our two old '64 Fords there. Once, while we had our show *Diamond Studs* running in New York City and had come home for a break, I recall a big celebratory gathering beneath the pines outside at Merritt's and tall, dark-haired Mississippi Delta poet Jim Seay saying, "I got something to show *you*: my ant-car!" and placing a small bearing shaped exactly like a Volkswagen onto the station's concrete foundation skirt and letting it roll forward, as vehicles of all manner had rolled into and out of Merritt's for so long.

When Jim Wann and his co-creators devised in the early 1980s the filling-station-and-diner hit Broadway musical *Pump Boys & Dinettes*, the model for it was Merritt's, and the laconic mechanics (who sang lustily: *We keep America rollin' / We're the Pump Boys*) of the show—Jim, Jackson, Mark, and Eddie—were really Tom and Ben Grantham and Dick Gibbs and, of course, the old turkey and coon hunter himself, Cap'n Eben Merritt, who if he walked into the place today would indeed still recognize his old station by shape and white stucco and terra-cotta roof and would marvel most appreciatively at its money-printing BLT-sandwich trade, yet who would also look about and wonder:

Where's that big sycamore tree used to be across the street?
Where're the gas pumps?

Where're the good ol' boys and the benches?

And where're my bananas in the sunny window, getting good and black and ripe just like I like 'em?

Whiskey Hill

One story that *never* got told at Merritt's Store but that I learned in recent years, oddly enough from my very favorite elementary school teacher, whose husband had been one of the veterans involved in it: In the very late 1940s, maybe 1950, when prefab Victory Village was new and flooded with returned World War II veterans and their families, one vet from Wilkes County, North Carolina, convened half a dozen others for a beer, sat them down, and said, "Boys, I don't know about y'all, but the prices at the state liquor store are 'bout killing me."

"Amen!"

"Yeah, man."

"Tell me 'bout it."

"Well," the Wilkes County vet went on. "I got an idea. Where I'm from, I know how to make the stuff, pretty good. If you boys'll go in with me, cost of making a still and all, we can set it up way out in these woods between here and the stadium. Nobody's ever out here, I'll run it off at night, and we'll all be drinking for just about *free*."

Every man came in on the deal, and very soon, as good as his word, the Wilkes Countian was supplying each of his cohorts with high-quality, high-octane white liquor. And so it went, successfully and agreeably, for about six months or so.

Then one of the other vets piped up at a gathering and said: "Now this is good stuff, don't get me wrong—but we've been doing some work with *flavoring* in my chemistry class, and I think I might could add in a little something and get it tasting maybe a bit more like real bourbon, say."

"Hey, man," said the Wilkes Countian. "Sounds good to me—you've been helping a right smart—you know how to do it: why don't you run us off a batch of 'bourbon'?"

All hands agreed to let him see what he could do.

Shortly thereafter, the chemist went out to the still, which was a good three-eighths of a mile from the apartments, in a small clearing among the hilltop white oaks and post oaks, reached by an almost imperceptible deer path, a perfect hiding place for these amateur moonshiners. He went to work with his flavorings in the mash and then put a fire under it.

And he promptly blew the still up.

And started a fire.

Not a small one, either—a forest fire, a wild fire. The chemist hightailed it away from there and, back at Victory Village, told his comrades to lay low and to say nothing.

Meanwhile, the fire raged, and every fire truck and pumper in Chapel Hill showed up and worked to put it out. Overwhelmed, they called in everything Durham could put to the task, and when these combined forces were still not enough, they enlisted a bevy of fire trucks and firemen from Raleigh—a five-alarm fire across three counties. Finally, the efforts of the college town and the two other cities together managed to subdue the blaze in the stadium woods, without further incident, the woodland being so large and relatively distant from the town of Chapel Hill itself.

As there had been no storm, and thus no lightning, to set off such a conflagration, the chief state arson investigators were called in, coming from Raleigh to look the scene over, and in short order they happened upon a few buckled barrel hoops and a charred boiler and an equally charred, distinctive copper coil: the worm. They had found the ruined still, they had found the cause of the great fire, and now they would find the human agents behind it all.

Neither of the SBI men had much of a notion that twenty-some-year-old college boys living in dorms fairly far away from this spot had been coming out and distilling illegal spirits here. They both, though, looked gimlet-eyed at the nearby married students' housing, full of grown men from all over, combat-hardened men to whom World War II had given all manner of technical skills and no shortage of confidence. Surely, the investigators figured, they would find the moonshiner fire-starters in Victory Village.

And so they knocked on every door, throughout the whole place.

"Sorry to bother you, ma'am—your husband around?"

"No, he's in class and the library till about four o'clock."

"Okay, you tell him we'll be back about then and we'd like to talk to him."

"Can I tell him what it's about?"

"Sure. We're looking into the recent fire."

On they went. Finding a man at home, the talk went a mite differently.

"Sir, you wouldn't know anything about a still being operated back up in the stadium woods not too far from here?"

"No, I sure wouldn't. Never heard tell of that."

"You positive?"

"Yes, I am."

"Nobody ever offer you any white liquor?"

"Not around here—there was one time in Gatlinburg when—"

"We ain't asking about no Gatlinburg. You never even heard of any white liquor being drunk by anybody in this place?"

"Nope."

"If you're lying, we'll put you so far underneath the jailhouse they'll have to pump air down into you."

"Sorry, officer. Don't believe I can help you."

So it went, all through the married students' housing—not one soul knew anything about a still, nor about the products of one. Nobody knew anything—everybody knew nothing. Nothing a man would own up to—not the men, nor the women either. There was one Wilkes County man who was certified terrified, along with half a dozen of his co-conspirators, but, mirabile dictu, not a one of them cracked. And the SBI men—knowing full well that, somewhere in that warren of deception, they had certainly confronted their villain and that he had bested them with an unbreakable code of silence, their repeated and intensifying threats notwithstanding—at last gave up, took the evidence back to Raleigh, and filled out the report: The stadium woods fire in Chapel Hill had been started at and by an illegal whiskey still deep in the woods, established and operated by person or persons unknown.

They kept the case open for a spell and returned to Victory Village several times, just to ask at least a few of those whom they knew to be guilty, or harboring or protecting the guilty, if they might have heard anything in the intervening months.

Still, no one had.

No one had run off any more white lightning, though. And everyone in Victory Village's Wilkes County gang had gone back to patronizing the state liquor store on the edge of town and paying the state boys those high state prices, the wages, as it were, of sin.

Title Search

The old hundred-acre Morrow Farm about a mile from the Schopler cabin had been in the hands of the same family for at least a century, and when Lizzie Morrow, the matriarch, died, that family put it on the market.

Eric and his wry and charming watercolorist wife, Miggie (whose English archaeologist parents had studied Tutankhamun's tomb at the time of its discovery in Egypt), took a keen interest in the property and invited me to come and walk the land with them. Owing, and thanks, to the example my

Hand-hewn log

outdoorsman father set for me, I have long believed the walk in the woods to be one of humankind's greatest gifts and pursuits.

Yes, of course, I said, and there we went.

The farm featured a couple of small, flat ten-acre fields, separated by a narrow grove of pines. My first impression of it was that the balance comprised mixed Piedmont woods, more pines, many very tall hickories, tulip poplars, a few huge oaks, and some gorgeous red cedars and hollies. Eric's main interest lay in those fields—he told me he planned to raise beefaloes henceforth and needed the land to grow hay for them. (Frank Queen warned me when he heard this news: "Beefaloes? They're bad to take out fences.")

The Morrow Farm lay upon the land, south to north, in the shape of a football-field rectangle, and as we walked the long way toward a great unnamed hilltop just beyond the farm's northern boundary—at 630 feet above sea level the highest spot for many miles—we came across several large sawdust piles, evidence of the workings of a portable sawmill in times past.

An old log cabin in ruins, its hand-hewn log walls eight feet up, its mortared stone chimney still in place but not its roof, stood in the pines just off the Morrow Farm's eastern boundary; years would pass before I discovered a set of dry-stacked, slender, flat stones in the leaves nearby, foundation for a long-gone shed.

We made this trek several times on succeeding Sunday afternoons, till Miggie Schopler phoned me one day and asked if I might accompany Eric, as she could not go today—and that if he went to the Morrow Farm alone, he would certainly get lost in those deep woods. She knew I had a keen sense of direction, so I readily agreed.

Perhaps that was the day we went through the woods a new way and found a logging lane that led toward the big hill's summit from the west and led us up a broad southwest-facing slope that I immediately took to, as we followed that log lane farther up, looking back down the not-yet leafed-out slope and, also, over into a broad ravine. On the far side of the ravine lay the bone-white stitching of an old split-rail cedar fence, collapsed upon itself.

Little other evidence remained of what in the early 1900s had been a hog lot—only, along the farm's west side, a line of ancient cedar fence posts with old staples (called "steeples" hereabouts) holding small pieces of brittle, rusty barbed wire. Timberman Glynn Fields had all but clear-cut the place in the early 1950s (during my title search, I would see his timber deed and smile, because I knew Fields well from Merritt's in south Chapel Hill), and the only stumpage he left standing were the cut's *exempted* hickories— just why I could not cipher. No one seemed to know, till years later one of Clover Garden's old timers told me, "Oh, hell, that was because Marvin Morrow was a *squirrel hunter*, big time!" In the seventy some years since that timber cut, a great many native species have grown up and back to surround those exempted hickories, the southwest slope booming with oak, beech, red maple, holly, dogwood, redbud, sassafras, bluets, pokeweed, red cedar, native honeysuckle, native azalea, persimmons, tulip poplar, wild iris, milkweed, all regenerating themselves by the hand of God. Some Elaeagnus and stiltgrass have snuck in, yet for the most part the land has acted independently as to what it wanted, on what the land and the land alone determined was, in Tom Earnhardt's words, wild native growth that was "not *optional*."

❀ ❀ ❀

A few more of these strong Sunday afternoon outings and I began to get my mind right, started feeling proprietary, became willing to entertain the notion of buying and building there, letting the bit fit, and so on. Soon Eric had purchased the whole Morrow Farm, and not too long thereafter he and I made a deal on the northwest corner's fifteen acres, that ancient hog lot, contingent upon a little legal work that I took on.

Great friend and mountain attorney Frank Queen taught me how to do a title search on this land, how to navigate the register of deeds office, and sent me into the fray with an encouraging flourish of: "Hell, you can do it yourself!"

So I then found myself up in the Orange County Courthouse in Hillsborough, thanks to Frank, pulling big ledgers across their rollers and studying what our record-keeping people had to say about my newly chosen Clover Garden hillside. My search was fairly simple: John Morrow, whose four-room cabin beneath giant looming oaks was in a shambles though still standing, had willed the hundred-acre tract to his son Marvin Morrow, who in turn had willed it to his wife, Lizzie, the matriarch, whose heirs sold it to Eric Schopler. A set of covenants written by Eric and Miggie (nothing to be subdivided below ten acres, no trailers) had been laid upon the land, and a common road-maintenance agreement would soon be in place as well.

Frank had me check out the lis pendens register to see what else, if anything, someone might have filed as a claim against the land.

I found none, though I did know of one fairly recent adversarial dustup involving the southern boundary of the Morrow Farm, nothing that would affect the property I wanted, to wit:

An older man from across Morrow Mill Road had come over to where Eric Schopler and dairyman Edgar Pickard were studying the front of the two flat fields and the farm's newly surveyed border. The older man, a pistol holstered on his hip, claimed loudly that the surveyor, whose nickname was Hedgerow because folks said he needed a hedgerow in order to shoot a straight line, had placed Schopler's south line, running along that front field, too far south, invading the older man's property on its north side.

What Eric and Edgar had been doing when the older man approached was plucking the surveyor's orange tape from pieces of broom sedge and restoring those lengths of tape to the surveyor's actual wooden stakes, right back where Hedgerow had placed them during the survey. Apparently this upset older man had, in the dimness of dusk or even dark of night, moved them to the north, away from Hedgerow's line, and he now came forth to challenge Eric over the line.

And armed to do so.

The man pressed his case hard and so did Eric, who said this is where Hedgerow had shot the line and so this is where the line was and would remain. The protesting elder did not draw his gun, Eric told me, though he did place his hand, hard and agitated, upon its holster, at long last turning on his heels and leaving the roadside scene with these bitter words: "Well, we'll *see* about that."

Eric, whose lawyer-father, mother, brother, and sister had left Germany for Madison, Wisconsin, soon after Hitler took power, was not about to be intimidated, though he did fill with anger. Edgar the dairyman, who had spent his whole life in the Clover Garden community and knew all its members and their ways, somehow knew nothing would come of this blustery set-to, and he calmed Eric with his stoical assessment: "Now look here, Eric—it don't mean anything. Anybody can come out and tie a ribbon around a damn *weed*!"

That fall, after Frank Queen had graciously read and approved my title search, Eric Schopler deeded over the Morrow Farm's northwest corner, the southwest-facing slope, and I was soon mapping out and building a lazy-C lane up the slope to the top of the ravine—upon which, once the lane had been cut and dozed and gravel had been poured, timberman Clayton Rogers (who always rode his tractor standing straight up and singing hymns full-out) and I drove up and down the lane to flatten the gravel down, all the while talking, singing, and sipping a little from brown paper cups he had stashed in his truck's glove box, with "Peace & Love" lettering and white doves decorating them.

Soon the road builders returned and cleared a three-acre field inside of that lazy-C.

And then, soon after celebrated author, *Paris Review* veteran, and UNC creative writing director Max Steele had hired me to teach at Carolina (once *Heart of the Country*, my novel of southern music—from the early hillbilly string band and blues era of the 1920s up to the last performance of the Grand Ole Opry in Nashville's Ryman Auditorium on the Ides of March, 1974—was about to be published), that left little to do but have a tin-roofed Cajun cottage built in the woods up above the field.

Once I moved in, about my nearest neighbors were, to the west, Clayton Rogers and his wife, Ruby, in their hilltop home high up over Cane Creek; and not far to the east, across the big woods of the early 1900s Gold Mine Tract, the family of Johnny Baldwin, a Black man I often saw and stopped to visit with, both along Gold Mine Road and at Jerry's corner store. It was Johnny who told me of people showing up from far and wide to sneak soil, subsoil, and stones away from the Gold Mine area, taking it off to be analyzed, some even taunting him (he did not own that tract and never troubled with it), saying, "We're carrying it off from underneath you, Johnny!" Johnny said he thought these unknowing trespassers (the mine was a bust and may have even been salted) were ridiculous: "They come from Lord knows where, dig all day, *deep* too, and go off with bags and bags of dirt and worthless rocks. They all of 'em think they're rich, but they got *nothin'* for all that work!"

So now I had left the Schopler cabin down on the creek for hillside living close by a tapped-out gold mine, but really for the big oaks and pines and hickories.

And for all the lovely maples on the hill.

William

The people of Clover Garden always warned against "putting up hay against the rain," an old country expression both literal and figurative, involving acute delay, getting way behind, and rushing and its dangers.

When partly wet hay that one family had cut and stored caught fire (spontaneous combustion from the hot, drying middle of the bales) and burned the roof off about a third of their main dairy barn, the short-statured patriarch, with his manure-encrusted overalls, hired a carpenter to put the barn back to right, and a couple dozen Clover Garden men volunteered to work under and alongside the carpenter, myself among them.

The work was straightforward, banging roofing nails all day long through the seams of galvanized tin.

How we ever successfully went back to work in the afternoon after the double-gracious-plenty midday *dinner* that the matriarch lovingly brought forth for all of us (chicken and gravy, pork chops, green beans, mashed potatoes, buttered biscuits all the way to the horizon, *and* custard pie), I do not know. We left her kitchen all of us round enough to roll right off the roof we were fixing, though, somehow, no one did.

I had known one of the barn-roof rebuilders almost since the moment I had moved into the Schopler cabin on Cane Creek five years earlier, because he occasionally showed up at the Schoplers' home just upstream from the cabin, honking his pickup truck's horn by way of warning, looking for a dram from Eric's well-stocked bar (and explaining why then, why there): "They don't know, back at the house, that I like to take a drink."

One sunset, the patriarch and I leaned on the corral fence outside his milking parlor and this normally quite humorous older man waxed oddly philosophical—he had earlier that day gone by a nursing home to see a good old friend, a fellow dairyman recuperating from having taken a severe kick to his head from one of his Holsteins.

"I been knowing him my whole life," the patriarch said, shaking his head, "and now he don't have no idea where he is, or even *who* he is. He don't even know *his own name*." The patriarch shook his head just a couple of times and hung it and did not speak again for a full minute, till at last he looked up at me and closed this moment, saying sadly, "You know, Bland—the years go by."

At the close of the noisy barn-rebuilding day, as I climbed down off the long roof and headed for my truck, the patriarch fell in behind me to see me off, following me across the barnyard as I walked to my truck, shouting out like an eighty-five-year-old man in a stockyard: "Jim, Jim, I can't thank you enough, Jim—really 'prechate all your good work, Jim!"

Big genial William Morrow happened to be standing nearby, leaning into his truck, putting some of his tools away, and he could not help but hear all this Jim-ness. He wheeled around and cried out: "His name ain't Jim—his name ain't Jim at all. This is Bland Simpson, lives down on the creek."

No way was the patriarch going to be upbraided and bested by his fellow dairyman, especially one who had towered over him by almost a foot and a half all their grown-up lives. He turned to William just as politely as possible, hands on the hips of his crusty outfit, and in the most unctuous tone I had ever heard from him said, "I know that, William. I know what his real name is. I just call him Jim because I *like him so much*."

And there was an end to it, though I do not know how I kept my truck on the road all the way back down to the cabin, I was laughing so hard at the sheer goofiness of the patriarch's calm, self-protective retort, which, though I do not answer to Jim, to this day I still dearly love.

A number of times in the first several years I lived in the Schopler cabin, I was with Eric when William Morrow, our dairying neighbor just to the west of Beechwood, would come around. William was a tall, ready, friendly man serious about how things ought to be done and done right, yet most always smiling, never didactic, and always warmhearted in his greetings and in the way about him.

The fall when I would turn thirty, I asked William if I might hire him and his flatbed truck with wooden sides to haul a small group around on my birthday—a hayride. He agreed, and when I asked further if we might stay on only four-digit roads (in North Carolina these were low-use tertiary roads, many still gravel), he laughed heartily and said, "I'll take you on roads ain't got no numbers and no names—*farm lanes!*"

What a good man, and, good as his promise, so he did—he drove a couple miles from the cabin, once we had all piled in, and went off-road down into the Cane Creek valley hollows and up on its hills, all this being well before the Cane Creek Reservoir was flooded and filled, and William knew all the secret lanes and cut-throughs, it seemed, between Clover Garden and Teer, and out of the hay-filled flatbed for quite some time that night came laughter and fiddle music, antique tunes alive as they ever were and really filling the air.

When the field within the lazy-C lane was being cleared and the tallest of the hickories with their high crowns came down, the ground shook, and I could feel those earth-shaking concussions in the soles of my feet a hundred yards away. The work took much of the topsoil with it into a set of long windrows right in the middle of the new clearing. I knew I needed to plant a cover crop or two and start to create new ground, and with good advice from neighbors close to the soil I chose *sudax*, a cross between sorghum and Sudan grass.

One afternoon William Morrow drove over from his farm on his tractor with a disc harrow barely narrow enough to fit down Morrow Farm Lane and started chopping and cutting into the new field's red-clay hardpan, while I followed him on foot with a hand seeder spreading sudax seeds out in a broad spinning circle. To disc and seed the whole three acres took us a couple of hours, after which we stood up top of the field at the big red maple and talked.

"What're you gonna do with those windrows?" William asked me, crossing his arms.

"Burn 'em," I said.

"Burn 'em?! That'll take *forever*," William said.

"Seemed like the cheapest way to knock 'em down."

William kept his arms crossed, turned his gaze, his big round face, from the windrows to me and back again several times, then looked beyond the windrows and spoke out toward the field.

"Now if a man wanted to, he could push all that trash on down into those lower woods. Get him a bullnoser for a day and move it on down. Then a man would have him a nice clear field, and he wouldn't have to wait but five, ten years for all that mess to rot away and settle on down. That's what a man might do."

"You reckon?" I said.

"If a man wanted to," William said, adding, "Well, I best get on back up to the house. Let me know when your cover comes up a little bit; I'd like to see it." Then, barely taking thirty dollars for his time and gas, he was up on the tractor and away.

That was in the spring of the year.

Over that summer, the sudax greened up the red-clay clearing quickly and William came back, looked in on the new field, and approved. Within a few short weeks it was nearly eight feet tall, and I cut it down with a two-cycle Stihl brush-clearing tool, a circular saw blade on a shaft, and the air was full of a bright, sweet, sugary mist as I did so, the sorghum side of sudax showing itself. By early fall it had boomed up to its earlier height again, and, after slicing it down a second time, I called William Morrow about coming back with his tractor and discing it in as I reseeded the field, this time with fescue and red clover.

When we finished this second planting job together that fall, again we stood up the slope looking out over it all, and when he saw me take my checkbook out, he reached over and pushed my hand down, shaking his head no.

"No, you just let it be a present—I'm happy to help you."

And then he paused, looking out to the west, toward the sunset. "You know, children are the best thing there is in this world. I don't know how anyone could ever think that I would want to hurt a child."

No doubt at all in my mind what he was talking about.

Though William and I had become great friends, we had never once discussed it; I had learned from Eric and from others, the way you do when you stay on in a place: an unavoidable accident years before; a child on a bicycle suddenly darting out directly in the path of his passing truck; the loss of a life; the deep, unassuageable grief in every direction; and vengeful recriminatory telephone calls to him in the depths of night.

William kept staring off into the hickory and oak and beech woods on the other side of the field, 300 feet or so down the slope from us, and I thought this noble man might advise me yet again about the windrows and the bull-noser and pushing them into the lower woods, but after a spell of silence his thoughts aloud went another, very different way.

"I tell you what I'm gonna do one day."

"What's that?" I said.

"Build me a cabin, just a little cabin, way up in the woods up back of Isabel's and my house, up toward the ridge top toward Austin's Quarter where I grew up, you know, where Charlie Bradshaw used to put his foxhounds out to run."

"Yes, I know right where you mean."

"Won't be nothing fancy, now—no electricity, just a bed, table, and chairs. A cooler. Kerosene lantern or two. And I'll go out there at Christmastime, stay for a week, maybe two." Then he turned and looked me square in the face and with deep, solid, sad intent said: "And there won't be no *phone*."

Trout

Not too long after my road and field were in, Eric Schopler soon built a two-acre pond on a very small stream flowing west through the Morrow Farm and stocked that muddy water with largemouth bass and bream. When he later grew discontented with only those selections, he decided that there was simply no reason why he could not raise top-of-the-line rainbow trout there.

Easy, he told me (he had studied up on it): just put fingerlings in a fine-mesh triangular cage, about four feet along each of the triangle's edges and about six or seven feet tall along the ribs; tie the cage to the cedar-post pier on the north side of the pond and sink it there; and feed them every evening with fish-food pellets dropped into that cage through a small door held shut by a waterproof bungee cord.

Eric was nothing if not a great salesman, and he roped me into this scheme—made a rainbow-trout sharecropper out of me. He would buy the cage and the fingerlings and the feed, which would sit in a metal can at the land end of the pier, and I would drift over and feed the trout of an evening. We would raise the trout over the cold months, November to March, and split the take once they were up to frying size.

All went well over the holidays, during their first two months or so in the water, and I went from being a bemused skeptic to a hearty anticipator: a red-clay aquaculturist! And of trout, no less! I took real pride in seeing the prized fish grow as I watched them relish the feed when I pulled the cage up partway above the surface of the pond waters, opened the small portal, and poured the pellets in.

Winter, though, even in this mellow part of the Upper South, has its tricks to play, and in late January or early February, we suddenly got most of four inches of rain over a night and the following day, and when I went down to the pond to feed the trout, the water had risen all over the pier decking and the cage had been pushed by the flooding waters up under the pier.

I knew right where the pier was and had no fear of walking out on it, though I could not see it—but the temperature was in the mid-thirties, and I needed some waders. So I drove a mile down to Dr. Fred and Marie Summers's home (Eric and Miggie Schopler again being abroad for a time), which was the old Morrow Mill itself, thinking he might have some waders to loan me. Which he did, chest waders with knee-high boots that he freely loaned me, wishing me good luck as I headed back to the trout farm.

At the pond, I half covered myself with the waders and strode confidently out upon the flooded pier.

The boots, both of them, immediately filled with frigid water, and, backing up, I saw in the wintry shine of my car's headlights what I had been too hasty to notice back at Fred's: broken dry-rot slashes up and down the boots, which had so easily let the cold water in.

Carrying several quarts in each leg now, freezing and disgusted, I still went sloshing out onto the pier to reposition the cage. As I wrestled it back out from under the pier frame, for it was heavy and awkward, I suddenly saw that the little feeding door was wide open.

Not a single rainbow trout of any size was still left in the cage.

When I returned the worthless waders to Fred Summers, who hailed from Iredell County most of the way to the high Carolina mountains where rainbows normally lived, he remarked wryly and with little concern: "Well, I never really thought this latest scheme of Eric's was gonna work. At least you won't have to keep feeding trout every night . . . for *nothin'*."

Just Folks

Even a small community like Clover Garden possesses a rather large cast of characters, when all the various familial relations get figured in, along with pals, employees, interlopers, husbands, wives, and ex-husbands and ex-wives, though a small *stable* community has blissfully few exes.

At the time of my move from the cabin up to the hillside Cajun cottage, or not long before, when the lane into the Morrow Farm was scarcely a timber

The trout pond that never was

road, a slender, dark-haired guitar-playing man lived in the old John Morrow farmhouse there—that turn-of-the-twentieth-century one-story, uninsulated, dilapidated dwelling so out of plumb, or *sigodlin*, as mountain poet Robert Morgan would call it, that my advice to Eric and Miggie, once they owned the tract, was to bulldoze it once the guitar picker had moved on down the line. The old place sat innocent of paint or insulation, and whatever the guitarist had done to improve it was not particularly evident—floorboards had gaps between them and lay there easily liftable off the joists. The guitarist's main contribution to the small-farm estate seemed to have been the laying of saplings into the long muddy trenches leading into the woods, and laying them lengthwise rather than crosswise like a plank or corduroy road. If not the guitarist, someone from his group of mates and stay-overs had named the place the *Kokomos*, because that is how any number of near neighbors referred to it, to me, after I was up in the cottage, as in: "You living at the Kokomos?" or "Are you *one of* the Kokomos?" And after I had answered *no* for long enough, the word "Kokomos" fell into disuse in Clover Garden.

One of the sunbeams of Clover Garden was Barbara Talbert, a happy woman with a solar-powered smile, who ran the corner store before Jerry Copeland did (and who was always kinder than kind to my young twins, from a previous marriage) and who only left the store to run a catfish restaurant just down the road apiece, in a cinderblock building that had been, in turn, a country store (where the man and wife who ran it played hearts all the time with their big companion and fixture, a man always in overalls whose only utterances—*ever*—were belches, earning him the nickname from Fred Summers's three daughters of *Mr. Burp*, and I recall feeling more than a twinge of real sadness for him after he had passed on and the volunteer fire department burned his farmhouse just down the road as a training exercise), a plumbing outfit, an electrician's shop, and then for a spell Barbara's restaurant. Everyone loved her and loved the fish house, yet there just were not enough fish-favoring folk to keep it afloat past a few months.

One after-sundown enterprise that did catch on for a spell in that same block building where Barbara's fish house had been was a beer bar and music club that did limited business till the owner, a local man, turned his stage over to troupes of *exotic dancers* several nights a week. The place was then always packed, if the number of cars parked cheek-by-jowl was any evidence. Clover Garden, I judged, was a fairly conservative community, though at least some of its people may have been loosened up to some extent by the adult amatory materials mail-order shop called Adam & Eve, operating in a windowless brick building across from the exotic-dancers emporium. A number of Bingham Township folk worked at A&E, and one older farmer told me, bemused, that he never knew what his wife, a worker there, might bring home to show him of an evening, once saying: "I came home last Thursday and there on the dining room table was a great big pink plastic pecker just a-lookin' up at me!"

This same older farmer also told me how touched he was that one of his granddaughters, a young woman perhaps in her late teens, had been invited to join one of the troupes of exotic dancers!

Not long after that, though, he told me of a family incident that disrupted the odd little country showplace.

The local man who ran it, at the height of his glee and cash flow, also had a local aunt, who on one much-discussed Saturday night came into the overflowing club and walked up to the onstage microphone, interrupting the dancers and the show as she shouted into the mike: "Sonny, you may be my nephew but just look at all this: you're the sorriest man in all Bingham Township, and I'm gonna go back outside and get in my big Oldsmobile and bash it into ever' single one of the cars parked at this club. You just watch now!" And with that she marched impressively right out of the club and the hundred exotic-dance enthusiasts who had settled in for a long night of it did too, suddenly all running for the door, all of them evacuating the club like a dose of salts.

Not a car on the lot, not even the nephew's, by the time the aunt got into her car and took her time and *aimed* it—only the brights on her Oldsmobile shining over and into the soon-dark building, which come Monday morning had a large sign hanging dolefully upon its door: *For Rent.*

Dixon the car-parts man, with his well populated junk-car arena out in back of his shop, worked a scant tenth of a mile across Highway 54 from Jerry Copeland's corner store. One would often see him golf-carting his way back and forth from his shop to the store for sodas, and I remember running into him once a few weeks after selling him, for a song, my '55 Chevy Bel Air four-door sedan, a car that, while parked near the cabin till I could find a good engine to replace the thrown-rod item in it, suffered a limb's falling upon its windshield, which spidered all out and made the car a dead ringer for the Generalissimo Trujillo shot-up death car, and that—in addition to the thrown rod—caused me to throw in the towel on that gorgeous work of art.

"Mr. Dixon," I said. "You took that '55 Chevy off my hands about six weeks ago."

"Oh, yeah," he said, remembering, "The windshield."

"Are you going to fix it back up and sell it?" I asked him.

"Nah," he said, "I had it crunched already."

"*Crunched?!*" I said, appalled. "But it was such a beautiful car!"

"It was *old*," Mr. Dixon responded. "Old is *bad*; new is *good*."

Then he paid for a soda and a pack of Nabs and left the store. His grown daughter Carol, who also spent some time driving the golf cart back and forth from the shop to Jerry's, came to have a very popular, highly respected, and much sought-after electrician's business in latter days, sometimes, I would reckon, changing old wiring out for new.

Ms. Rebecca Crawford—a fine cellist, tall, older, still mostly a strawberry blonde—lived not far from Teer, the very small dairying community several miles north of Clover Garden, right on Cane Creek, and she performed in all manner of events near and far and was just as kind and sweet-natured as could be, the cello seeming to have given to her expressive gestures. She drove a large station wagon, its wayback big enough when the rear seat was down to accommodate her cello. I saw her down at Jerry Copeland's one afternoon, pulling in, cello in back, and spoke as she got out of her car: "Ms. Crawford, how are you doing?"

"Oh, my Lord, honey, you haven't heard?"

"No, ma'am—what's happened?"

"Nothing *now*," she said. "But last month I went out on a walk in the woods—alone, the more fool I—and I was way back in there and I tripped over a tree root and sprained my ankle and couldn't get up and even if I could, no way I could've ever walked two more miles out of those woods. Nobody knew where I was, and don't you know I lay there all night long and most of the next day. A good friend of mine, a man who checks in with me every day and sometimes walks that trail, when he couldn't reach me in three tries figured out, 'Well, maybe Rebecca went out for a walk and *something happened!*' Which it did, of course, and don't you know he came right out and walked the trail till he came to *me!* And I said, 'Well, I'm mighty glad to see you, though it sure took you long enough!'"

"I'm so sorry to hear about this, Ms. Crawford," I said.

"I tell you what: that's something I don't *ever* need to do again, and I don't recommend it for *you*, either!"

I saw Rebecca Crawford some years later in a grocery store produce section in town, where she was gathering up a gang of cucumbers, and when I hailed her she told me she was there after cucumber sandwich makings for the next day's Daughters of the American Revolution meeting in Chapel Hill.

"My aunt Evelyn Burdette is a member," I said. "Do you know her?"

"Evelyn Burdette, Evelyn Burdette, oh I just can't *live* without my Evelyn Burdette!" Ms. Crawford practically danced and almost dropped her cucumbers as she sang out my aunt's name so extravagantly.

When I phoned my much-loved aunt Evelyn and told her of this brief encounter, Sister, as we always called her, was simply beside herself with laughter. That exhilarating moment among the cucumbers was the last time I saw Ms. Rebecca Crawford, the lovely cellist from Teer.

Once, a preacher from the area, a man who did programs, speakings, and even musical shows far and wide beyond his own church here, asked one of his flock to join him in the latter, saying he needed a rhythm instrument to go along with his energetic one-man-band trombone playing— could she join in with him and play tambourine?

She thought she could, she said, and the comments and reviews from their first few Sunday afternoon and evening shows were excellent indeed, and so the preacher accepted, sought, and solicited more shows, increasingly distant from the Clover Garden area. Which meant that the preaching trombonist and Sister —— the tambourinist were spending more and more time together and getting back home from these Sunday outings later and later.

Then came the day of reckoning, when the both of them suddenly left the membership and the area, together, so it seemed, their careers having grown more entwined, as they had too, over the months devoted to all those far-flung shows. The tambourinist's muscly husband had finally put his big Cat's Paw–heeled foot smack down on the traveling band.

No one seemed to know where the disappeared ones had gone, and there the matter sat, out of time, out of mind, for at least thirty years.

Till I happened through a small eastern North Carolina town, and out of the very corner of my right eye I saw the runaway preacher's full name on the marquee board in front of the church, though I missed what the proposed message for the upcoming Sunday was to be.

Yet that preacher and the tambourinist had already left a strong message, a parable even, concerning the Seventh, Eighth, and Tenth Commandments, behind in Bingham Township, and so I saw no reason to stop and inquire further.

The man who could do and fix *anything* in Clover Garden was Raymond Kirby, a trim, lithe, handsome man with a ready smile and a great friendliness about him—he always came around soon after a call to change out a lock, clean a chimney pipe, or pull out and replace a used-up dishwasher, and he never seemed worried, hurried, vexed, or bothered about a repair situation, however large or small it was.

Once when I had missed seeing him at the cottage, I stopped by his brick home down on Highway 54 not far east of Jerry's corner store to write him a check for his work. I pointed at his Pro-Line cuddy cabin fishing boat, under a tin-roofed shed out back, and asked him if he were getting out much these days, and that query prompted a small flood of enthusiastic reports of places in and around coastal Carteret County he and his wife, Gwen, liked to go.

One spot in particular was an older one-story motel with some boat slips on the west side of the Atlantic Beach causeway. They would go out and fish in Bogue Sound, maybe come around past the freighters' turning basin and the Coast Guard's Fort Macon and fish in the sound behind Beaufort Inlet, the old masonry fort on one side and Shackleford Banks on the other.

And then come back to the motel after a day of it on the water, clean the fish, relax . . .

And grill.

"They've got grills right outside the rooms," Raymond told me. "Old-style, really nice feel to the place. You know what I mean?"

"Yes," I said to one of the happiest men I have had the pleasure to know. "I really do."

The first thing I learned about Oliver Pickard, another big, genial man of few words who lived alone just off Morrow Mill Road, was what a fine craftsman he was: Miggie Schopler showed me the elegantly simple wooden curved-top breadbox Oliver had made for her.

The second was that a poisonous spider had once bitten him and sent him to the hospital. Eric Schopler, visiting him there, told Oliver he sure was sorry about the black widow bite's laying him low, prompting Oliver to let

Oliver Pickard's former home

Eric know how so many older women were coming to the hospital to see him, all of them courting him by bringing him cakes and such: "That black widow's nothin'—it's all these *white* widows that're what's botherin' me!"

One Saturday morning, Eric and I drove over to the Big O Jamboree between Eli Whitney and Saxapahaw, a popular bluegrass showplace (Bill Monroe and the Bluegrass Boys would play there) that held a no-less-popular flea market on the weekends (housewares, tractor implements, old board games, rusty trucks), and we soon saw Oliver in the crowd, or *over* it, as he stood head and shoulders above most everyone.

"Well, hello there, Oliver," said Eric. "What're you looking to buy here today?"

"Why, not a thing," Oliver replied.

"Oh," said Eric, laughing. "Why'd you come over, then?"

"To see," said Oliver, simply and proudly, "and be seen!"

For the longest time, the small auto repair shop on the rise just east of White Cross carried the name "Larry's" and had as an emblem a smiling golden teddy bear and the phrase "Authorized Bear Service"—whatever that was. Well, *Bear Service* must have been something sure-enough good, because that was more than fifty years ago, and the shop still serves those of us who live out in White Cross, Clover Garden, and Bingham Township, now under the name of "Sturdivant's [Larry's last name] Tire Pros," operated by the wry Terry Sturdivant with his convivial front-office partners Danny Scott and Blaine Sturdivant, George Clack, and a host of top-tier mechanics: Jeremy Wade Talbert, Ward Whitfield, and half a dozen others. Jeremy Wade's father, Garry, a masterful towing-service operator with whom I have been friends almost the entire time I have lived in the community, has kindly pulled our family's vehicles back to Sturdivant's from troubling situations hither and yon forever.

If one commutes to the university in town, if one tours professionally with an Americana string band, if one pulls a small boat as my wife, Ann and I long have done to far-flung locales and roads that run down to the rivers and creeks of eastern Carolina, with its convoluted 10,000-mile estuarine shoreline, to explore and report on the exotic spots, one needs excellent analysts for one's prime vehicle (which best not give out at a swamp river landing a mile down a sandy lane). As the title song to *Pump Boys & Dinettes* declares: *"We keep America rollin' / We're the Pump Boys."*

In the musical, that chorus salutes gasoline dispensers working at a small Gasso station, based on the very real Merritt's Esso in Chapel Hill. Like old-time Merritt's, Sturdivant's has exactly the same number of bays, with ancillary fair-weather repair areas. And the men there are, and have been for years, not only wrench-spinning analysts and fixers . . .

They are also our friends. They tell it straight about problems they anticipate from my descriptions, about problems that might be surprises, about faulty relays that kick the respected and even feared *Check Engine* light into its orange illumination—relays that are themselves the problem and not the vehicle itself. If they say, "You're fine to run up to Asheville on those tires, but I'd change 'em in the next couple months if I was you." Or, "That left rear tire's all cupped out and you don't want to be running on a rim by Saturday night. How about let us go on and change it out?"

Bravo's Market, White Cross

One can count on their word. And then the word one truly wants to hear, whatever one has brought the car in for, is Danny simply calling out in his high, clear voice: "You're *ready!*"

Bravo's

For a time, the log building at White Cross was home to Piedmont Feed and Garden, till that popular plants, birdseed, and horse-feed emporium outgrew it and moved a mile and a half west toward Clover Garden. The log building sat empty for years, till an enterprising woman nicknamed Harry made a modest variety store of it and named it for herself: Harry's Market. When she put a small post office in one corner, we thought she might have found the key.

Yet a scant year later, Harry's folded.

Another several years of desuetude.

Until Bravo's.

Bravo's Market, straight across the two-lane blacktop from Fiesta Grill in White Cross and selling "*productos Hispanos,*" opened in early November 2019 to modest fanfare, plastic colored flags, and a winking-lights sign that announced its twelve-hour days. Inside: piñatas, ceramic moons, and foot-tall models of Mexican women and men, and also all manner of tortillas, dried beans, *cervezas frías*, gorgeous produce, locally sourced Crawford Dairy eggs and frozen meat and Maple View ice cream and milk, Carolina Brewery Copperline amber, a rack of wines and champagnes, and a steadfastly cheerful woman named Maria running the place and always reminding one of "tamales on Sunday!"

Bravo's was fully stocked, truly homegrown, a small but still legitimate grocery store, and from the moment it opened the only one in Bingham Township in southwest Orange County, all twelve miles wide and most of twenty miles tall. At no other grocery anywhere that we knew of could one park no farther than ten or twelve feet from the front door.

We very much wanted it to succeed, as we had when a parallel operation, Fiesta Grill, opened across the highway fifteen years or so ago—as many a restaurant had quickly come and gone there, including a pizza parlor and a variety-show cooking spot that offered international takeout dishes from twenty or more countries: "Any dish on earth!"

Chewy, the steadfastly cheerful Mexican American soul who had opened Fiesta in the small Butler barn, had succeeded with generous chimichangas and modest prices, so the place stayed packed at lunch and dinner almost from the moment the orange neon "Open" sign first showed itself at White Cross, a truly successful, long-term, and swiftly beloved restaurant.

Could Bravo's do the same?

Maria in an odd downbeat moment told us a day or two after Christmas that first year, "No gente," or, *no people, no one showing up,* and so we began a word-of-mouth campaign in the Clover Garden community, asking our neighbors to stop at Bravo's now and again and stock up, spend fifty dollars whenever possible. Many others were also spreading word, and the campaign soon seemed to be working, for Maria brightened when we came in one Saturday afternoon and told us that the Valentine's baskets, huge armful affairs full of chocolates, a bottle or two of red wine, and heart-shaped cards and decor, had moved briskly, one of them with a price tag of seventy dollars! She beamed and announced that there would be more baskets at Easter and Mother's Day. This was promising and welcome news indeed; things seemed to be picking up, and our colorful new local grocery has hung on and continues to offer us community coherence in the rolling forest- and pasture-land west of town.

It came to pass that the COVID-19 pandemic made Bravo's a most fulfilling, full-service grocery, with comparatively low contact compared to far larger emporia, and its custom has steadily grown: *Brava, Bravo's!*

As we would leave in those early months, saying "A la semana," Maria would smile and bid us to return soon, always saying farewell jauntily: "Tamales on Sunday!"

The Pharmacist Who Fooled Them All

Not far southeast of White Cross, at a curve in what is now named Carl Durham Road, stands the old two-story farmhouse where Carl Durham was born in 1892. He went to county schools, studying at home by candle and lantern light, and then went on to study pharmacy at UNC, becoming a pharmacist's mate in the Navy during the Great War and a popular, longtime pill, philters, and potions dispenser at Clyde Eubanks's drugstore, with its tall Toledo Scales ("No Springs, Honest Weight") front and center, on East Franklin Street in downtown Chapel Hill.

Durham was active in Democratic politics and got himself elected to the Chapel Hill Town Council and the Orange County Board of Commissioners, and then, in 1938, without having raised his hand, an unusual political thing occurred that changed his fate.

That year, after three terms as a congressman, future US senator and North Carolina governor William Umstead declined to run again for Congress in North Carolina's Sixth District, and Democratic leaders at opposite ends of the district quickly found themselves at loggerheads as they split their support over two different candidates.

The split proved intractable, till the two party leaders decided to table their differences and delay a knockdown, drag-out fight till 1940, when they planned to find a man for the long term upon whom they could agree. Meanwhile, they determined to put a straw man on the ticket to "hold" the seat for two years and two years only.

"Let's put Carl Durham in there for the moment," one said, and the other quickly agreed. Likable Carl would do that for the party.

And so Eubanks pharmacist Carl T. Durham went on to carry the Sixth District in November 1938 with over 75 percent of the vote.

Congressman Durham was a New Dealer, championing the Rural Electrification Administration, which had only sent its first lines out into country North Carolina in 1936, by 1940 reaching 24 percent of the state's farms, and by the mid-1950s lighting up almost all of them. The congressman knew what it was like to live in the near-dark.

In 1940, when the Sixth District bosses came back to Carl Durham, with the new man they supported together in hand, and asked the congressman to step aside now, they found that their White Cross country boy turned out to like the Potomac River political world just fine and told the bosses he believed he would stand for Congress another time, hardly what they expected or wanted.

As incumbent, Durham carried the day again, and the bosses who had put him into Congress as a placeholder would never ever be able to prise him out and retrieve that seat—he would serve eleven terms, precisely twenty-two years, from January 3, 1939, till January 3, 1961, stepping down of his own accord after reaching the position of chairman of the Joint Congressional Committee on Atomic Energy during the first full decade of the Cold War.

So never underestimate the power of a modest, well-liked country pharmacist to change his mind during his first congressional term and claim for himself the seat that others thought belonged to them. Congressman Durham was a child of the horse-and-buggy world of Bingham Township, and he had known since boyhood exactly how to hold tight to the reins.

The Mysterious Sculptor of White Cross School

The old plain and simple brick schoolhouse at White Cross, built in 1933 and closed in 1961, as one of the last such consolidated schools left in the county, was declared by the Orange County Board of Commissioners in 2015 to be a "local historic landmark," and since its closing as a school I have seen it be, or serve as, many things, to wit:

1. The headquarters of the North Carolina Writers Network. At a celebration day there once, I heard a woman ask the late "Ol' Fred" Chappell, one of our state's most prolific and admired authors, if, as a teacher, he thought he had ever given wrong advice to a young writer, whereupon he answered, "Oh my God, yes—I gave some bad advice to *you*!" and where that night, when many folks were dancing to a strong, throwback R&B playlist, I saw John Shelton "East Tennessee Slim" Reed and his late wife, Dale, dancing outlandishly well, as if they were still in high school.
2. The headquarters of Child Care Networks, a clearinghouse for parents seeking help, where once I performed a short set of songs as part of a fundraiser for the group, even inviting our twins, Hunter and Susannah, onstage. They walked on with balloons to such crowd delight that they did not want to make an exit (thus bringing to mind

the comedian W. C. Fields's stringent stagecraft advice "Never work with dogs or children").

3. Once or twice an actual day-care outfit.
4. A long-running vintage store called Furniture Follies, which featured throwback 1940s and '50s yard pieces like lime-green gliders and other low-budget wonders made of bright slender piping and springy seats, in which we invested delightedly, heavily at times, though Ann's mother, Pat Kindell, once asked: "Where'd you get all this junk?!"

Yet of all the endeavors for the old spot, the most truly intriguing operation I ever witnessed at White Cross School was when the very large central portion of it served as the art studio for the first-tier sculptor William Emsley "Bill" Hipp III.

From the moment Hipp, a devilishly handsome and keen-eyed man not yet thirty in the late 1970s, greeted Eric Schopler and me and we stepped through the door into his atelier, his world, I felt a deep sense of wonder about the scene Hipp had created in which to work: easels, pedestals, tables, boxes of plaster, mounds of clay and wax, steel smoothing spatulas eight or nine inches long, bolts of cloth, all not so much arranged as simply set and settled in place by a master craftsman who knew where everything was and would be when he needed it, regardless of how willy-nilly this great room might look to the casual interloper.

Hipp and I shook hands, and I stood aside while Eric gazed upon the bust-mold of his firstborn son, Bobby, to be cast in bronze, which Hipp was sculpting for the Schopler family. I took it all in, feeling in those moments that I had been borne back to a wonderful artist's studio in Paris or New York in the late nineteenth century. Surely Bill Hipp had a lady nearby, his mistress, his wife, a painter herself perhaps, waiting maybe beyond that hanging canvas divider with grapes, a baguette with brie, and wine to begin their evening together—the time was already about seven o'clock, nearly dark. And surely he and I, fellow artists out in the southwest Bingham countryside, might have occasion to confer from time to time and salute the arts, the drive to create, the lust for life, the passion of it all . . .

Yet these fifteen minutes turned out to be the only time in my life I ever saw and spent with Bill Hipp.

Though I saw his work displayed in places of respect: busts on the UNC campus he had been commissioned to do—Justice William Bobbitt, Senator Sam Ervin, Institute of Government founder Albert Coates, playwright Paul Green (other castings of whom stood outside the Waterside Theatre in

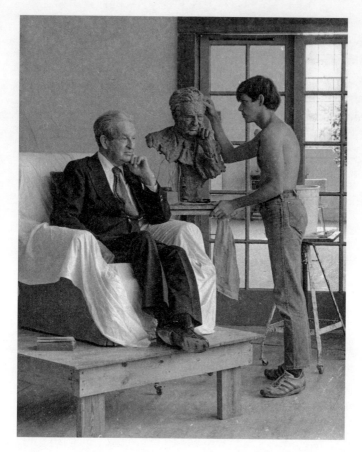

Playwright Paul Green sitting for sculptor William Emsley Hipp III, White Cross School, October 1976

Manteo, where Green's *Lost Colony* had been performed since the summer of 1937, and in the lobby of the Paul Green Theatre at UNC). All of these busts resided in Dialectic Hall (New West) and Philanthropic Hall (New East) on the University of North Carolina campus, the meeting places of the Di-Phi student literary society, of which I had been a member and which I have long advised.

A Bill Hipp bust of Thomas Wolfe gazed over the Morehead-Cain Foundation lobby, in the observatory building near its sundial and rose garden on East Franklin Street, and one that Hipp sculpted of Carolina's extraordinary basketball Coach Dean Smith sat in honor at the Smith Center—the Dean Dome—on South Campus.

Farther east, New Bern honored its early eighteenth-century co-founder with the presentation of Bill Hipp's now-weathered bust of Baron Christoph von Graffenreid, set in place on Pollock Street downtown on a base of Mexican granite on April 9, 1989.

Nothing in this record thus far gave any indication of Hipp's psychological difficulties or of his star-crossed, long-lost love, who would memorialize him in a 1997 newspaper piece in the *Greensboro News & Record*, alternately romantic and clear-eyed as she looked back across twenty-five years, over his trail of disaffected and, later, fearful friends (one of whom recalled the sculptor's once drinking—*chugging*, if not *shotgunning*—two dozen cold beers during the relatively short one-hour drive from Asheboro to his White Cross School studio) and his descent into alcoholic and schizophrenic madness.

What she would far rather remember, clearly, was this idyll she painted of spending time with him at the White Cross School: "I'd fly south, to another college town, Chapel Hill, to sit on the veranda of his country studio, listening to the night frogs in the trees, smelling the perfume of the roses and gardenias he lovingly tended."

John Sanders of Johnston County—twice director of UNC's Institute (now School) of Government, reformer of the consolidated UNC System, redrafter of the North Carolina Constitution—had counseled other Dialectic and Philanthropic Society members on Bill Hipp's quality work and helped with Hipp's commissions, and he knew Bill Hipp far better than most. He told me of tracking Hipp down after he had left White Cross and Chapel Hill, finding him living in a remote portion of Columbus or some other southeastern North Carolina county, visiting with him briefly there, and then learning in 1991 that Hipp had gone missing.

One day on the UNC campus about 2000, John Sanders stopped me and told me with certitude that he just knew Bill Hipp was dead.

"*Dead?*" How did, or could, John know?

He thought Hipp's body must have turned up by now in the East River. And Hipp's college and then long-thereafter lover, Charlotte, author of the 1997 remembrance—upon learning that no one had heard from Hipp in years, not since that last-time-seen day in summer 1991 when he left North Carolina for New York with $5,000 in cash that he said he had just collected on a debt—said: "I knew he was dead. . . . Something had happened to him, there in Manhattan, a homeless crazy man on the street with a big wad of cash."

Was that the dreadful and simple end of it all for William Emsley Hipp III of Davidson, North Carolina? Disappeared: his last known act of calling his grandmother (collect) from a phone booth in New York City, missing for years and now *dead*—for sure, for true? Whether by his own hand and purpose or that of another, who would ever know?

I thought of the dashing, confident, poised, and archetypal artist I had met briefly that long-ago evening in the White Cross School.

And I thought of him, too, recalling Marlowe's *Tragical History of Doctor Faustus*, the final chorus ringing out this sad report and clear warning: *Cut is the branch that might have grown full straight . . .*

Jehovah's Witnesses

Few folk, excepting my late longtime neighbor Mr. Stacy Thompson, ever came back as far into the deep woods as our place and field, till years ago when a cadre of Jehovah's Witnesses (at the start, about five of them, four large middle-aged women and a short stout man with a flattop, all in a Chrysler K-car that he drove) started driving the eight-tenths of a mile from the hard road back to the Cajun cottage.

Just as nice as could be, all of them.

They would leave off a *Watchtower* and visit briefly, letting me know that the end times were still hanging in the balance and would be on the way pretty soon.

About every six months, the Jehovah's Witnesses would visit.

They were unfailingly quite kind and had a winning innocence about them, by my lights, and their end-of-days prophecies never bothered me (the sun will explode in about 5 billion years, so, of course, they were right), so I liked them. In time the crowd dwindled down to just two women who kept coming way back here faithfully for quite a spell.

Ten years.

Once I heard someone calling out happily to me across four checkout lanes at the Carrboro Plaza grocery store: "Mr. Simpson, Mr. Simpson! Jehovah's Witnesses, Jehovah's Witnesses!" and I recognized the longtime visitor and waved back gratefully.

That was the only time I ever saw (or *witnessed*) any of them anywhere else but back here at the cottage. The last time the two women showed up, I had just locked the front door and was walking to the car, late afternoon, and I was off to meet someone in town.

Yet here they came.

I greeted them and then one of thumped a Bible with spirit and then said, "Mr. Simpson, we'd like to talk with you today about the *book of Revelation!*"

All Pentecostal and what I have heard some people call "off-brand" denominations love Revelation with its mystical, if not crazed, images and predictions, worshippers seeming to believe the book gives them all manner of permission to interpret the truly bizarre work as sense and fact, as accurate, detailed, literal prediction of the days to come.

"Well, I'd love to," I said, and I meant it. "But not today. Today I'd rather talk about the book of Ecclesiastes. My favorite."

"Didn't I tell you?" one of them immediately shouted at the other. "Didn't I?"

"Yeah," the other said, sorrowful and downbeat. "You did."

"I *told* you, I *told* you! I just *knew* it. I just *knew* he was gonna want to talk about Ecclesiastes."

And then they both in turn very politely said they were not prepared to talk about Ecclesiastes on this day. "We'll have to come back for *that*!"

They thanked me for the short visit and drove off, and that was the last time (the *end* time!) for a very long while that any Jehovah's Witnesses ever came a-visiting. But their seeming foreknowledge about Ecclesiastes and me made them all the more likable, of course, and made me love the old lyrical King James prose and its wisdom with affection anew.

As the Preacher in that truly and deeply Good Book says: *To every thing there is a season, and a time to every purpose under the heaven.*

Mr. Stacy

Mr. Stacy, who had once very graciously given me a slow-walking tour of the early-1900s Gold Mine Tract and the mine site way north of his house, when out on foot always waved at passing drivers with one slowly lifted right index finger. Whenever I drove past him, more often than not I would stop, roll down the window, and visit with him for a few minutes.

Though I never once saw him over my way, much of a mile from his home, he would tell me, familiarly, things about my land, about the pair of turkeys he had seen not far from my house the last month, about how nicely he thought the rain came down my driveway, slowly down the lazy-C curve around the field, and about how much better that was than if the drive had been built to go straight up the slope. He was most of eighty, had lived in Clover Garden all his life, knew every shortcut and stream, every rock and rill in the woods, and constantly roamed over it all, "scouting," as he put it, just to know for himself the true, literal lay of the land.

If my small twins, Hunter and Susannah, he a towhead, she a redhead, were buckled into my car's back seat when I stopped, Mr. Stacy would always lean in through the window and take a good look at each of them, back and forth, and then remark: "Say them's twins?"

"Yes sir, Mr. Stacy."

"Don't look nothin' alike."

"No sir, they really don't."

"Sure don't," he would add. "Not a thing alike."

So Mr. Stacy walked everywhere in Clover Garden, had no car (maybe he had been in a bad wreck long ago, people wondered, though who really knew?), and I might see him out on NC 54 at Jerry Copeland's corner store or at Lewis Allen's store, maybe even over on the road up to Orange Grove. I often offered him a ride, though he would always wave me on—except once, when he rode with me into Carrboro and asked me just to let him off at the tire store across from author Lee Smith's Akai Hana sushi bistro.

Would he want a ride back out to Clover Garden in a while?

"That'll be all right," he said, meaning no. "I'll find somebody going back out. Or I can always walk."

And that is how he was remembered at his funeral service in the small Clover Garden Methodist Church, on the oak-grove hilltop with the long view past its graveyard over the cattle and horse pastures, too, off to the south.

"Mr. Stacy was a *walking* man," the young preacher proclaimed. "A *walking* man!"

And people nodded and murmured and smiled. Mr. Stacy was a walking man indeed, all the way up to his death at eighty-seven, and no one else in the community was even in second place. Out on the hard roads of Clover Garden, he had no competition, nor did he in the deep woods where he was always out scouting and was never seen.

"I asked him," said the preacher, "after I learned he'd never been to the Atlantic Ocean, over and over: 'Won't you let me drive you to the Outer Banks, or Atlantic Beach, so you can *see* the Atlantic, walk a little on the sand?' But he always said 'No.'"

Folks nodded, for they knew what was coming.

"Must've asked him for a *year*, thought he ought to at least see the Atlantic, close as we are to it—till one day he told me: "'Now, preacher,' he said. 'You know I was in War Two, out in the Pacific.'

"'Yes sir, Mr. Stacy, I know you were.'"

The congregants looked straightaway at Mr. Stacy's flag-draped coffin.

"'And they all tell me,' Mister Stacy went on, 'that the Pacific's twice as big, or something like that, than the Atlantic.'

"'Something like that,' I agreed with him," the preacher recalled.

"'So if I've seen the Pacific, the *big* one, why on earth do you reckon I need to go see the Atlantic?'

"Well, he had me there," said the preacher. "And that was the last time that I *ever* tried to get him to go down to the Carolina coast with me.

"God bless Mr. Stacy. He was a walking man, amen."

Amen.

And I think most of us in the sanctuary that March day said *amen* twice.

Speaking of Lewis Allen's Store

Lewis Allen's store out on NC 54 had served as Clover Garden's post office for a year or more, while the bridge over Cane Creek at the old Morrow Mill (the one where I had found the great horned owl) was out for replacement. Mr. Allen, crusty though he was, had even earlier done our neighborhood a real service by welding an old fuel tank onto an angle-iron tobacco sled to create a pig cooker, an oven on wheels that I went in on, one that would acquire a name—the Centurion—and quite a reputation around the township for good and efficient pig-cooking (whole hog or shoulders, scorched to perfection, we liked to say).

One time Jake Mills had a flat tire out Clover Garden way, close to Lewis Allen's garage. I cannot recall if he took the flat off his car and changed the tire or just limped the car into Allen's, but either way he went to see if Lewis could get it recapped.

Lewis Allen took one look at the flat tire, with the steel-belted metal in the radial all sprung out to glory, and turned back up at Jake and pronounced grimly: "You 'bout got the *good* out of this one, son."

Since everyone knew Lewis Allen and his store, his name came up often and, at times, in unexpected ways in Clover Garden community talk.

One afternoon, I went over to see my neighbor Frank Morris, the saw-miller, who lived across a long horse pasture from Mr. Stacy, the *walking man* of our community. I was there to ask him about the cottage (which Frank's brother Bennie owned) that stood right inside the nearby fork in the road, leading everyone to call the place "Bennie in the Crotch." The place was just then for rent, and my dear old friend Homer Foil, a fine actor with a beautifully clear-tone tenor, was interested in it, and so I was inquiring.

Barn at the heart of Clover Garden

Frank was about seventy then, and he and another older man were standing in Frank's driveway, close to the road, and shortly after I arrived, apropos of nothing I saw or heard, they suddenly started in talking about sex, in the same laconic, matter-of-fact way they might have spoken of the weather, or working up firewood, or who they might have seen just driving slowly down the road in a truck.

The other man, whom I had never laid eyes on before and have not seen since, said, "Well, if I'm going to, you know, *be* with a woman, I'm only gonna have *one* drink, not three or four, I can tell you *that*."

Frank nodded sagely and looked off beyond the big faded-red barn full of hay and the great oak trees surrounding it, considering this comment for a bit and then slowly offering wisdom of his own: "I tell you what—nowadays I'd just about as soon have the *promise* of it as it *itself*."

They both turned to me, and I nodded in good faith, smiled, and said nothing. Then Frank asked me: "You know Lewis Allen, don't you?"

"Yes, sir, I do."

"Well, you know about what happened the morning after he got married?"

"No, sir, don't believe I do."

The other man apparently did know, because he was already smiling.

"Well," Frank said, "I think you moved out here too late to know Joe Ray—"

"I know the Rays near me, and down toward the Old Greensboro Road."

"That's his people," said Frank, "but he died about 1960. Anyway, he was a good man, a *working* man. And the morning after Lewis Allen got married, Joe Ray drove his truck down early to the station, same one where Lewis and his wife live now, over top of it, and that's where they were then—and Joe Ray parked out front and got out and honked and honked his horn and shouted out, 'Lewis Allen, Lewis Allen, I got something to *say to you!*' till Lewis finally came to the window and threw it open. He was in his twenties, Joe Ray about fifty then.

"'What is it, Mr. Ray?' Lewis Allen called down, and Joe Ray reared back and said, "'I just want to tell you, you got any *fancy lovin'* you plan to do, you get it *done* by the time you're *forty!*' And then he got back in the truck and drove on off. That was Joe Ray."

The best talk that I ever heard down at Lewis Allen's store, though, came a good while later, one cold, sunny December afternoon between

Christmas and New Year's Day. I stood inside, waiting for Eric Schopler to collect his mail from Mr. Allen. A young woman walked in, passed me, and asked Lewis Allen for directions to Buckhorn—she had missed the turn—and I only vaguely listened in. Then, having heard Lewis Allen state the way (up past Cane Creek Baptist Church, just above Orange Grove, turn left), she passed me again, stopping at the door, turning back toward me straight on, and then saying: "I know you."

Her musical voice now caught my full attention at once, and I saw the light in her eyes and immediately realized who she was: Ann Cary Kindell, whom I knew from The Nature Conservancy and whom I had not seen in nearly three years, and then I said four of the most important words I would ever say in my life—for later the next year we would begin courting in Washington, DC, where she then lived, working at the Conservancy's national office, and on a Christmas Eve within two years' time, we would be married: "I know you, too."

PART 2 ❁ *When Ann Came*

When Ann came back south—she had grown up in Sea Level, Down East, Carteret County, North Carolina—to make a home with me, from her high, steep wooded hill overlooking a branch of Rock Creek and its park in northwest Washington, DC, to our hillside cottage in Clover Garden, she brought with her several slips from a lavender azalea bush there in Cleveland Park, which have all thrived here, and many flights and flocks of goldfinches.

Azalea brought from Rowland Place,
Cleveland Park, Washington, DC

Goldfinch on coneflower

I saw the finches suddenly one summer's day, all over the ground of our field-side yard where we had thrown some birdseed, and where no finches had ever shown themselves before. The yard, the leaf litter, the oaks and hickories nearby, all turned gold that summer and fall, for the small song-birds were here everywhere, en masse, and they did not leave us.

Soon we set a cylindrical feeder out there, with thistle and black oil sun-flower seeds in it, and sometimes these small black-and-gold wonders seemed to be on the thistle feeder all day long. At other times, a batch of them might be on the ground below, going after seeds that had fallen down, and if one of us opened the door to the deck, there would go half a dozen goldfinches, flying up into the trees inscribing as they flew an ephemeral cone of gold. To see one chase another, the chaser staying right on the tail, and trail, of the chased, this was hard to keep up with, so agile were they. Now and again one would balance itself on a tall yellow-flowering weed near the porch, which would lay way over under the goldfinch's weight but would not break.

Everything they did seemed charmed and gorgeous.

And to see as many as twenty or thirty of them take off up out of the grasses in the field: what grace and a grand, awe-inspiring sight, too.

We tried all manner of baffles to keep the gray squirrels at bay from the feeder, but none ever worked—several plastic ones, they just plain ate. At last we discovered a broad, ridged black metal baffle that sat not fixed but loose upon a metal collar on the thin pipe that held the feeder aloft. A squirrel might catch the edge of the baffle, but when he threw his weight upon it and attempted to climb it, it would dump him off; none of them could ever get enough grip and traction (what a mountain man I know, describing his car working hard to get up his steep driveway, calls "gription") to mount it and ascend to all that dark seed.

Early one summer morning, Ann and I were sitting on the screened porch watching the house finches, two new families we thought, hog the feeder, boxing the goldfinches out, as the early morning grew darker by the second. I had just five minutes earlier added sunflower seed to the feeder in a very light rain—now, as the darkness grew acute, a heavy rain simply blasted down out of the sky, laying mists into the woods and clouds into the field. No thunder or lightning: this one was a soaker, or rather, a drencher, lasting a half an hour and dropping the temperature maybe five degrees.

Somehow a hummingbird managed during the deluge to hold steady and feed at the flowers of two rocking three-foot-tall stems—a nodding onion and a blackberry lily—and how this least in size but strongest of wing pace withstood the downpour to do this, we could never know, but we smiled together and said all-praise to it in the moment.

Big Frank Morris, the sawmiller, came over with his tractor and harrow and disced up an eighth-of-an-acre garden and absolutely would not take a dime for it. That was right when younger daughter Cary was born, June of 1992, and Frank, done with the discing, the sodbusting, the smoothing out, said simply: "This'll be for that new baby—you and Ann, you just grow her some good stuff."

So here came the corn, rows and rows of it, Silver Queen of course, and rows of okra—Ann brought on all of that and the new baby that this produce celebrated. The now seven-year-old twins, Hunter and Susannah, loved it,

Hunter and his peanut crop

(*opposite*) Old Morrow Farm fence line

eating Contender and other bush beans right off the plants, okra right off their stalks, too—Hunter even boldly put a bunch of peanuts in the ground and grew several big batches of them, *perhaps* the only peanuts ever grown in Orange County, this far west of the fall line.

And Ann brought us a Christmas caroling party with the large Red Clay Ramblers family, with whom we ofttimes roasted a bushel or two of salty oysters and later put a reggae beat behind "We Three Kings" and "God Rest Ye Merry." Once a snowy white Christmas began right while we were singing one of the carols, and the band—Chris Frank at the piano, Clay Buckner and A. C. Bushnell on fiddles, Jack Herrick on trumpet—all shifted seamlessly into the great Irving Berlin ballad, and as the children shrieked and played in the snow outside, there were joyful tears in every eye.

She brought our annual New Year's Day walks down to the southwest corner of our land, where a scattering of dark-gray lichen-covered boulders lay, upon which the children loved to climb and play, and our strolls along the old fence line—those leaning cedar posts with their rusted and broken wire, memories, or even remarks, on most of a century past—running from our southwest corner by those rocks up to our northwest corner, marked only by an iron pipe set down into an old, now-long-gone white oak stump's depression.

Whenever the fescue in the field got cut, the children would pile it up, swim in it, poke their heads, only their heads, up out of it to be *people of the hay.*

Susannah seemed to love this part of her country existence, almost as much as the grazing she did, which we only learned about when Hunter came around the corner of the house one day saying, "Susannah's not *really* supposed to eat the hummingbird food, is she?"—a question that solved at once the long-running mystery of why a white lawn chair was often drawn up below a red feeder hanging from a small oak branch: she had been climbing the chair, tipping the feeder, swallowing the dripping sugar water. Often when young Cary was home without anyone to play with, she would spend the afternoons walking the perimeter of the field over and over, making up voices for different imaginary characters and telling original stories to herself.

Susannah holds Cary in newly mown field

Hunter loved kicking the junior football back and forth in the field in fall, after its second mowing, and, always, running down the field at least half a dozen times, I keeping my eyes on a stopwatch, he always striving to beat his own best time. And Susannah came to see and love the field as a spiritual place, which raised its value for us all.

We took slips of myrtle from Ann's father's Core Sound–side home in Sea Level and planted them at the top of the field here, where they and a yaupon cutting from Beaufort all flourished. We brought stones up out of the ravine and piled them near the myrtle, and soon Ann made a short field-stone wall for a rock garden, for flowers and herbs, for peonies and the tall light-purple Margaret Mills irises that Anne Mills Henkels culled from her Thunder Mountain hilltop home (they were named for her South Carolina grandmother) up near Orange Grove and gave to us.

And that small garden was for rosemary, too, especially rosemary, as the Bard's Ophelia reminds us, as she has done for over four centuries now: *There's rosemary, that's for remembrance.*

Buddy Boat

Jake Mills's aunt Katherine owned a farm bordering Burlington's City Lake, a few miles north of that town and a scant half an hour's drive from Clover Garden, and on occasion we went up that way to drop by to say hello and visit with her. Once I noticed a fellow a short ways off from us who seemed to have taken extra interest in Jake and me as we walked across a field to check out the farm's pond and talk about fishing.

Looking back at him, Jake said his aunt had told him that the man, a tenant of hers, was not quite right.

"He comes out to the edge of the field," Jake said, "armed with a long cardboard carpet tube and holds it up to his mouth and calls out through it, so it'll echo way off like a horn: 'Hey, goddamn! Heeeeeeey, goddamn!' He'll stand there half an hour at a time doing that. Sound like good sense to you?"

As we got ready to fish that pond together for the first time (where we would catch a few crappies), Jake pulled out his pocket knife (he always said that anytime anyone asked him if he had a knife, he replied: "I got my pants on, don't I?") and laid a big six-inch scratch into the side of the brand-new, Army drab green, Memphis-built jonboat (Desoto Manufacturing's "buddy boat" model) that I had just bought and that Jake had gone with me to Raleigh to pick up—before we had even unloaded it.

This was one Friday in May, and we had just put his trolling motor in near the bow.

"Why'd you do that?" I asked.

"So now you won't have to worry about your brand-new boat getting dinged up," he replied, "'cause now it already is."

We came back with shotguns between Christmas and New Year's, after ducks this time with Jim Seay too, crouching down in the dark 6 a.m. marshes near the lake, till at first light we realized the mists were so heavy we would scarcely be able to see a thing, even if any ducks flew—which they most assuredly did not. The venture was just too appealing, too tied to my love and faith in my father as an outdoorsman and waterfowler, and so I had fallen into those passions and overridden my lifelong awareness of how dangerous cold, wet weather and air were to me, and so paid for being enmeshed in that gorgeous, frigid morning with Jake and Jim by being brought down by asthma for almost two weeks.

But that misery would not start till later in the day.

So on the ride home Jake told us about another duck-hunting venture he had been on, years ago out on Pamlico Sound. He and his lifelong friend Steve Coley, a fireman, had gone down east and had supper the night before the hunt in a little Mann's Harbor clam shack full of other hunters, and one pair—in madras pants and penny loafers, and Jake said they didn't look or sound like they'd ever been hunting a day in their lives—were putting out a lot of loud bragging noise: "'We gonna *get 'em* tomorrow! Yeah, we gonna get 'em *tomorrow!*'" That sort of thing, generally making obnoxious fools out of themselves.

"Very early the next morning, 5 a.m. at the soundside ranger station where everyone drew lots to see what duck blind they would get," Jake said, "the loudmouths from the previous night drew the blind next one over from ours, seventy-five yards or so away. And at first light they starting blasting away: *Boom, boom, boom! Boom-a-loom-a-loom!* Nothing flying, but they kept shooting, boxes of shells, *boom, boom, boom-a-loom!* And Steve and I couldn't figure out what they were shooting at, till Steve said, 'Damn, Jake, it's a good thing they can't hit anything 'cause now they're shooting at the few snow geese that *are* flying!' Back then it was illegal to shoot a snow goose. And finally, after all that endless shooting, they *did* hit a goose and one started shouting, 'I got him, I got him!' and the other one shouting right back, 'No you didn't, I got him!' And then they splashed out to where it had fallen, both of 'em still arguing about who shot this illegal goose.

"Well, they picked it up and called it quits and went on in. And so did we—it was a bluebird day, nothing flying but the snow geese. We got to the ranger station to check out just behind them, and they stepped up to the ranger and got his attention with their illegal bird, still arguing as the ranger asked them: "'Sir, did you shoot this goose?'

"'Yes, sir,' one of them said proudly.

"'No, you didn't, I did,' said the other. The ranger was trying very hard not to laugh. For their deed, he could have seized their guns, whatever cash they might have had, *and* their vehicle.

"'Well, then,' said the ranger. 'I'm going to have to give you a $500 citation.'

"'You hear that, you hear that,' said the first one, beaming. 'I'm gonna get a *prize* for this great big sonofabitch.'"

Jake and I would take the jonboat down to Big Flatty Creek in south Pasquotank County on a couple of subsequent years' May weekends, motoring over from a state wildlife ramp and making a fish camp at the creekside end of a lane on my family's swamp timberland there and making good use of the ancient Sears "Ted Williams" 7.5-horsepower, air-cooled engine that

Shannon Hallman had stored out in his barn and almost never used, and so gave it to me for the buddy boat.

Our bounty was always and only bream and catfish, and that was aplenty—we would clean them and fry them up fresh in the evenings on an old two-burner Coleman stove.

As the former piney woods and small tobacco farmlands of Chatham County slowly filled and became Jordan Lake south of Durham and Chapel Hill, we would take the jonboat out there and push it around with the Ted Williams engine. Jake was an endless source of fishing stories involving himself, Steve Coley, and Bear Webster, for whom he and Steve had both worked hopping curb at the Oak Grove Cafe in Burlington. And usually when we stopped fishing just to drift and eat our vinegar and peppered sardines and saltines, peanut butter and cheddar cheese, Jake would bless our store lunches for covering all four food groups ("Sugar, salt, grease, and dirt") and would dish out such Merritt's-style riffs as: "You know why if you take a Baptist fishing with you, you've got to take two?"

"No," I would say, and I would have to believe whatever answer he might come up with, for as Jake often boasted, he had seen the "original Egyptian darkness" once at a county fair, or at least the big urn where the huckster said the darkness was inside of (though he refused to open it up, lest it get out).

"'Cause if you only take *one*, he'll drink up all your beer!"

We made a fair number of those ever-delightful treks, sometimes over to Horton's Pond not far from the big lake itself and where bald eagles circled in and landed on pine branches and fished from there. Then, as that long decade wore on, I took the big invitation to go touring all over America and Canada, Europe, North Africa, and the Middle East with The Red Clay Ramblers at a particularly busy and industrious time for the band, which would include scoring—both at our home studio and at NOLA Studio in the penthouse of the old New York City Steinway Building on West Fifty-Seventh Street—Sam Shepard's first feature film, *Far North*.

High times indeed, yet also a very long time when the jonboat mostly sat in our Clover Garden woods, full of rainwater, the engine sitting, too, in the cold crawl space under the house.

And by the time Ann and I had wed, on Christmas Eve 1988—in the Horace Williams House on East Franklin Street in Chapel Hill, serendipitously straight across the road from my beloved Page grandparents'

longtime home (the Robert Baker Lawson House, at the southeast corner of East Franklin and South Boundary), and also where Jake had lived right after he had gotten his PhD at Harvard and come back to teach at Carolina, once sitting under the massive magnolia tree there with a pitcher of gin and tonic and reading Cormac McCarthy's inaugural novel, *The Orchard Keeper*, on one single Saturday afternoon—and then taken off in January for an eastern North Carolina honeymoon, I do not believe Jake and I had been fishing, anywhere, for about two years.

For Ann's brown Subaru wagon ("Rooskidoo," she called it), I fashioned a roof rack and put the jonboat up top, turned-turtle style, all our luggage and the Ted Williams motor inside the car, and Ann and I were off for a fabulous week of cold winter boating on the Pungo, the upper Alligator, the Cashie River, and Pembroke Creek, coming back to the landings at dusk, lashing the boat up top of the Subaru with stiff, difficult plastic cords, and then enjoying all the eastern hospitalities granted us at the River Forest Inn in Belhaven, the Tranquil House in Manteo, and the Governor Eden Inn in Edenton.

Yet when she and I put the boat into the Pungo River at the Leechville bridge ramp for the very first outing of that phenomenal trip, I suddenly realized that I had not cranked the motor at all for two years now, and an ice-cold fear ran through and over me as I pulled its starter rope once—nothing—pulled a second time—nothing—but then just as suddenly that fear died, and I was singing hosannas to the Creative Power of the Universe, for on the third pull, that trusty old Ted Williams engine came through for us and absolutely leapt and roared to life with almost as much Pungo passion as our own.

Storms and Snows

As well as Ann and I knew coastal storms—nor'easters, gales, hurricanes—from our Sea Level and Elizabeth City childhoods, in early September 1996 we really should have feared Hurricane Fran more, when she rushed ashore near Cape Fear as a Category 3 and marched so quickly up the Cape Fear River valley. She brought us ocean rain, nine inches of it, on top of the five inches (*twice* the normal) of August rain we had already gotten—the two weeks before Fran's arrival had indeed been the archetypal "unseasonably wet."

All night long, what Ann and I heard were sticks falling in the woods and onto the tin roof—a whooshing rather than roaring sound through the night—and whenever I awoke I thought: *We're getting off light!*

What we could *not* hear, though, were the big trees going slowly over, uprooted from the soaked ground, if not noiselessly then at least quieter than

Fran's winds. Here in Clover Garden, the woods were not breaking so much as lying down, dozens of trees over the lane between our cottage and the hard road, a wreckage that took a squadron of neighbors with chainsaws and tractors days to clear, and then, with power out for over a week, the only place imperative for anyone to go was the only place with ice, to help folks sustain whatever food they had been able to hold onto: Jerry Copeland's corner store, two miles distant. Jerry was always amenable to letting you cash a check over the cost of the gas you had just pumped, and when asked how much over you could write it for, he always smiled and answered semi-cryptically: "Any 'mount 'cept Rocky Mount!"

Sometimes after such a big blow came odd rewards: an out-of-place egret at William Morrow's two-acre pond, hopping around on the pond's south edge, as if it were looking for breaking waves and surf and marshes on the sound side. Sometimes flights of seagulls by the 5,000 count: surprising, though somehow not unexpected.

When one lives out in the country at the very end of a particular set or trunk of electric lines, as we do, one finds that the power goes out often, at some times for a day or more, at others just a matter of minutes or hours. A squirrel might arc over transformer contacts at a substation and blow it out; ice breaking and bringing down lines will surely do it, just as heavy snow will too. Lightning might strike and fry a transformer, and we always keep a watch for heavy, hail-bearing thunderstorms and squall lines here on our Clover Garden hill, no less than we all do when we are out on the Carolina coast, and we always hold our breath when lights flicker, especially when they blink twice or thrice, both of us looking at once toward the drawer that holds the candles.

Sometimes the sky grays slowly from the west, and on comes a soaking rain, for which all praise and no fear. Yet sometimes after a few dead-still minutes, with not a breath of air, the temperature drops and the western sky goes a blue-black dark very quickly, and a thunderstorm driving over the land soon powers through, moving at thirty or forty miles an hour of ground speed and with raking gusts up to sixty miles an hour, making the pine trees swirl violently like they are being stirred about by the hand of God, shaking the house and woods with thunder, and dropping big hail ferociously. When these powerful storms would beset us, often making the children cry when they were young, we would as quickly as we could get out and collect some hailstones and bring them to the children to let melt in their mouths, advising them that this would make them *cousins of the thunder* and thus immune to the storm: no harm would come to them.

Still, no amount of hailstone inoculation has ever allowed us to escape the deafening cracks of thunder, day or night, and the immediate fear it brings, because we would know the lightning that had created it was nearby. And when calcium-white flashes coming in quick succession were so strong and terrifyingly bright enough to awaken us, with pounding, rolling thunder close behind, we would know the lightning striking might be less than a mile away.

And since the unnamed 630-foot mountaintop just above our cottage was the highest point for miles, we also knew well, though we might have it otherwise, that lightning was always already invited by the elements and by the land itself to come ahead on, 300 million volts right our way, to the high spot that has welcomed the great fierce power of king-hell ions for eons.

So snow has always seemed much to be preferred over thunderstorms and hurricanes, with its gorgeous unifying mantle, and how we love it when "the snow is general" across the land, as James Joyce put it. School is out, work is out, and the sled comes out of the shed.

I drove into Chapel Hill and picked Hunter up one evening during the winter of 1996, a snowfall just starting.

"Do you think it'll stick?" he asked with hope.

"No," I answered, "not at all."

At home a couple of hours later, he called me up to his bedroom window, from which he pointed down at an upside-down flowerpot sitting on the picnic table—the snow was already as deep on the table as the pot was tall, about six inches.

Next morning the snow was well over a foot deep.

Quite enough to pack it down on the slope of the field and make a sled run. Even after the field snow melted next day, the snow in the partial shade of the canopy on the lazy-C lane lasted, got damp by day and froze by night, and Hunter was able to slide luge-like from the top of the lane up by the cottage almost halfway out to our mailboxes, almost a tenth of a mile—he rode down over and over, shifting his weight in nuanced ways to increase, impressively, the distance he could cover, till a slight rise at a curve beside a huge short-needle Virginia pine (a wet early-January snow would bring it down years later) would allow him no more.

Snow could be a caution too. At least a couple of times, a barrage of snow came down, heavily flattening our two enormous ten-by-twenty-foot azaleas, collapsing each whole construct down to no more than a foot tall and giving us no hope for their recovery. Yet to our total surprise they came booming back to at least six feet tall in the spring.

Many a time we have left a car up at the hard road, which after most snows would always be easily passable a day, or even days, before our mile-long lane might be. Although, if we forgot to move a car, or just chanced it, what was so bad about being snowed in? And often neighbors would help, whether their efforts were sought or not.

Clover Garden, it seems, has long been that way.

One snowy morning not long after sunrise, when I was at the cottage tending to the twins on my own, I heard an engine chugging up by the ravine, opened the door, and saw deeply kindhearted, neighborly James Bradshaw up on his tractor seat, blade down (he had plowed the lane all the way back to here), smiling and calling out: "Thought maybe you and your twins might like to get out sometime!"

As I think back with a weather eye, there was one thunderstorm that got an uncritiqued pass from us, late on a May Saturday afternoon shortly after Hunter and Emilie's simple, elegant wedding service before a wooden arch in a little forest cove at the lower end of our field. Frank Queen came running over to me, saying energetically: "M. B., take a look," and thrusting his cell phone's dark weather page at me, "'cause this is what'll be happening *here* in fifteen minutes!"

A huge, swift thunderstorm now over Alamance County next door would indeed soon be drenching these proceedings. As the sky over the forest's western wall went to bruise-black, the bride and groom's well-dressed fellow New York City millennials freshened their drinks and got all mobbed up beneath the big tent and soon there was no talk at all, for the downpour in the woods crashed about us, making way too much noise for anyone to hear anything else but the thunder-booming storm itself.

And then, just as quickly as it came, the tempest blew away in a rush off to the southeast, and we all emerged again when a woman called loudly: "*Rainbow!*"

Yet arcing before us we saw not *one* rainbow but *two*.

A photographer urged Emilie and Hunter into the clean late-day light left by the storm, posed them in the field alone, the groom a southern man in a light poplin suit and the bride a Danish woman in flowing white: hands and hearts across the waters. Only 120 or so folks stood in an out-of-frame horseshoe around them, with that double-rainbow against the dark retreating clouds above and beyond them, the Lord's promised blessing caught there with them in a stormy, redemptive moment none could have expected, yet a moment everyone who was inside of would remember forever.

Clover Garden Dogs

We went to the animal shelter not long after Cary was born, and Susannah picked out the black-and-white border collie mix puppy we called Taba. Mix, I say, since he was hardly the size of a border collie—within six months he had the big, boxy head of a Saint Bernard and weighed a hundred pounds.

One morning when Jake Mills came out and Taba bounded toward him, Jake said, "Simpson, what have you done to ruin your life?!" Laughing, as he judged in the moment that once again I was living with livestock, but still . . .

Taba was as kindly a dog as one might want, and he seemed basically unaware of his size and weight. When we stayed in the small former net house near where the waters of Taylor's Creek and Gallants Channel meet in Beaufort and boated the family around—Ann and me, the twins, young Cary, and Taba—all in the fourteen-foot jonboat, we learned quickly that every shift of Taba's weight meant a forced realignment of all our selves, as the big dog's movements from side to side, even a sneeze from him, could make the full boat tip one way or the other, and the buddy boat was a creek boat with only a modest amount of freeboard.

He liked going over with us from the net house and its little beach to the short sandy beach on the western end of Town Marsh, which locals call *Cape Carrot*, after Carrot Island at the other end of the Rachel Carson Reserve complex of dunes, forests, marshes, and creeks. So in the summers of 1993 and 1994 we all got used to quickly shifting toward the opposite side of the boat from Taba's most recent move.

The children were growing too, though, so to obviate a life of maritime herky-jerky weight-shifting for all of us, we went in with my fellow Red Clay Rambler Jack Herrick and bought a Boston Whaler seventeen-foot, a Montauk hull and a significantly beamier and heavier craft than the little creek boat, and all was well.

Taba was so large that he really looked just right when he was out in the center of our Clover Garden field: a hundred-pound black-and-white dog almost three feet at his front shoulders with eighty-foot hickories and oaks behind him stood smartly in good stead and even had a certain woodsy nobility about him, running the three acres from end to end when it suited him, trotting alongside us as we walked the lane in the evenings. A grand companion with an impressive warning howl.

Then the dynamic changed.

Cary declared when she was about ten that "as much as I love Taba, I can't put him in my lap—I want a little dog I can do that with."

She studied small canines endlessly, got books with photos of them, and learned their names (most of them breeds, like the Brussels Griffin, that neither Ann nor I had ever heard of) and traits, and she and Ann stopped by various animal shelters in Chapel Hill, Mebane, and Oaks, coming home with excited, precise reports of dogs seen, liked, considered—once even a very large bluetick hound that they wanted me to see. When I did go see him and he gave a houndish *boof* and lifted up and put his front paws upon my shoulders in companiable fashion, I asked only, "What's *small* about this small dog?"

The afternoon came at last, in the late spring of 2003, when I heard the cottage door open and Cary and Ann say simultaneously: "We think we've found *the* dog!"

Quickly they pulled up a photograph of a Pomeranian on a screen—a golden dog stood proudly before a light-gray collapsible backdrop, neatly groomed and looking something like a chow dog to me; with nothing in the photo to show scale, this animal could have been two feet or two inches tall. Beneath its photo was the legend "Traits" with only two listed: "Friendliness" and "Incessant barking."

Cary and I were assigned to go back to the Chapel Hill shelter the next morning and check this potential dog out—a breeder had turned in two Pomeranian parents and three siblings, too large to be show dogs for the breed, we surmised, and of the siblings Cary fancied the only female.

Out she came from a pen, and we spent ten or fifteen minutes with her in an enclosed yard, and she was bright and active and did not bark a single time. Cary looked winningly up at me, and I said, "Let's take her home."

When we called Ann at her School of Government office, she was totally surprised, saying, "But I thought you'd turn her down!"

"She's wonderful, though. Was I *supposed to?*"

"No, no, I just thought . . ."

And so we got a small dog, five pounds or so to start, soon to be a little over ten pounds, one-tenth the size and weight of Taba.

Turkey tail

June (Cary named the little Pom for her birth month) took to Clover Garden life, with so much trotting and running that we soon called her breed a Woods Pomeranian, and in time her bright white coat acquired just a bit of a red-clay tint.

Taba was anything but delighted by her presence, and he went through four months' worth of phases, starting the moment she appeared:

- July: totally ignoring
- August: snout-rolling June away whenever she came near him
- September: watching her and acknowledging—admitting?—she seemed to be here to stay
- October: grudging friendship

✿ ✿ ✿

We all had to look out for June in her deep-woods home as she got acclimated, for once, when Cary and I let her out early in the morning, a large owl flew not four feet above her, checking her out, and we gasped.

Another time, down at Schopler's Pond, she went into the murky water as a puffed-out Pom and quickly shot herself out as a drenched white muskrat. Never again, that much was clear.

In the kitchen, she did backflip after backflip, yipped with delight, and was the circus dog we had always wanted, even though we had never known it.

Sometimes when I was at the piano, June moved in underneath the keyboard, beside the pedals, and barked and barked at me as I played and sang, distracting me enough at last to advise me simply to *stop*: she had had enough country rock and that would do for the day.

In Beaufort, when we walked down the street toward Taylor's Creek and turned to the right to head for the Gallants Channel turnaround at the western end of Front Street, June would have none of it; she must turn left, *only* left, toward downtown and the Beaufort Town Docks, where she could and would meet her public, all the children *oo*-ing and *ah*-ing over her and wanting to touch her, while their parents and grandparents made similar admiring high-pitched sounds and laid blessing iterations upon her: "Hey, Puff!" or "Why, she's nothing but a cotton ball!"

Taba, the reliable gentle giant, walked along a step or two back, like a footman of old, till age and arthritis took him away at fourteen and we buried him and planted a yaupon tree on top of him in the field.

And then, with only June, longer travel away from Clover Garden was possible for us, and we tried her out on a mid-March, weeklong houseboat trek on the upper St. Johns River in Florida (a trip that singer-songwriter James Taylor's late mother, Trudy, had recommended to us during a Chapel Hill visit, telling us vigorously of her varied pursuits, including: "I've piloted a houseboat!"). As we cruised up and down the gorgeous black jungle-lined stream, our tableau was one or the other of us at the helm and June, from ignition on to ignition off and the engine's low constant rumbling, flattening herself ruglike near the forward door so at the very least her doleful disapproving self could get some air. Not ibis nor alligator nor anhinga stalking the riverside shallows could gain her attention one whit.

At home, walking the lane with June one afternoon, Cary dreamed up a young-adult mystery series set in Paris, with a heroine modeled after Myrna Loy's Nora Charles in *The Thin Man* black-and-white film series, except a good bit younger, more like fourteen or so. And the heroine had a dog, a Pomeranian, modeled after Nick and Nora's Asta, and the series title was to be something like: *Michelle Donelle and Her Pom Named Pomme.*

With our inflated yet authoritative border collie mix, Taba, and our putative circus dog-detective Pom named June, we realized in all those moments over many years just how lucky with dogs we were, and that felicitous notion translated meaningfully into how lucky with life as well.

A Forest Home

In the run-up to that May wedding of Hunter and Emilie's, I had painted many things (the door and crossbeams to our garden shed, balusters on the stairs inside) that had gone more or less happily unpainted for years. This was all good, though one does get into oddly contorted positions when cutting in sash and trim, and the associated twinges can serve as muscular versions of Proustian memory prompts and transport one to similar events from far and away earlier times.

I got to thinking of the time my close brotherly fellow musician John Foley (later in the original *Diamond Studs* and a co-creator of the Broadway hit *Pump Boys & Dinettes*) and I painted a huge house in Durham one summer. Foley and I had priced it at a good fee ($600, above materials, worth about $4,500 now), and we looked forward to the couple of weeks or so it would take to do it.

A night or two before we started, though, Foley came over to me at He's Not Here, one of the yet-abiding Chapel Hill saloons, and said, "I told Bill H. he could come in on this with us."

"What?!" I said. I barely knew this Bill, but I knew that having another partner would cut our personal takes by half.

"Look," Foley said, "we *have* to let him—he's desperate—he told me he's been down to selling *blood.*"

Well, that was it, I reckoned—and so be it.

Foley and I rented some massive scaffolding in Durham's then decidedly untrendy warehouse district, got it moved to the house, set it up, bought the paint, and then, once everything was ready to go, here came Bill H., desultory but present nonetheless, and we all went after it, Foley and I on the scaffolding, Bill on a high ladder on a nearby back wall.

Late June, hot as hell. The house had a fortune of windows, all of which needed reglazing—after two days, we were much of the way down these two massive walls, and early on the morning of the third day, not fifteen minutes after we had gotten started, we heard Bill climbing back down his ladder. He stood silently below the scaffolding staring, if not glaring, up at us, and Foley said, "I'll go see what he wants."

I kept painting, watching them sidewise as they talked for only a couple of minutes, after which Bill walked on around the house and out of sight, as Foley came back up the scaffold.

Foley reported: "Bill says he just doesn't like painting. He said, 'Hell with this—I'm going back to selling blood!'"

This house-painting project finally took an entire month to finish, and I am not sure that we, as tradesmen say, *came out* on it—though we enjoyed the half-hour drives, singing Van Morrison songs, to and from our temporary farmhouse home that summer out on Mount Carmel Church Road south of Chapel Hill, and many evenings of croquet on a summer lawn did us good. We did have good company on the jobsite occasionally—two young boys from the neighborhood started showing up late in the mornings, while we were high up on extension ladders, telling us jokes and stories and laughing and after a while shaking our ladders from the bottom, while calling up to us for dimes. What for? we asked, and they would yell: "Chickensticks!"

And we, rattled quite rhythmically, would oblige.

Several years later, John Foley told me we needed to go say hello to Bill H. at his new place down in Chatham County not too far from Chicken Bridge, the Big Rock, and Frosty's Trading Post, and so we did.

Bill H. had given Foley excellent directions. We parked on the road shoulder beside a mature forest and walked the quarter mile straight back into this deep oak and hickory woods and easily found Bill's place.

The octagonal tree house, perhaps twenty feet in diameter, he had built entirely around a large central oak tree, its modest appointments a bed, a small kitchen, a few bookcases, and a woodstove—all at least twenty feet off the ground, the impressive structure supported by angled cantilever struts. All in all, inside the look of the captain's cabin on a sailing ship.

No plumbing anywhere in sight.

We climbed up a swinging chain ladder one at a time, the sort that pitches you backward as you pull up, and entered the tree house through a trapdoor, then sat on cushions and heard Bill's tale of building this elaborate folly, even in mid-decade already an ode to the 1970s. Having thus touched base, John Foley and I bid Bill adieu, climbed down, and left after our half-hour visit, the last time I ever saw the man.

While there, we also learned that Bill H. was not alone and that he had invited and convinced a woman *with a baby* to stay up there with him, raising groceries and diapers by a sort of rope-and-platform country dumbwaiter through the trap—though for all that, we never did find out exactly what he was doing just then to make a living.

Grilling

In the late 1980s, when I had first begun to call upon Ann in northwest Washington, DC, she would most always lead me up to a small grocery on Wisconsin Avenue, there to pick up some chicken or a cut of beef to grill back on the open porch at Rowland Place. Almost all our suppers had a grilling component, and I was appreciative and awed, even, at how familiarly and deftly Ann ran the operation, getting the coals fired up and the meat seasoned and on the grill, and how with her skills and experience she needed only to touch the upper side of the meat to know how rare or well-done it was. Having grilled perhaps only a couple dozen times in my life, I quickly realized I was going to have to step it up and learn how to cook over coals to Ann's specifications—for my experiences with the big multi-cooker barbeques at Orange Grove, where a dozen outspoken advisers were always present, were not going to help me now. A story came to us from northeastern Carolina, just after our first New Year's Eve together, and the tale helped me better understand the discrete world of holy smoke I was now entering.

Thirty years or so ago, not very long after a Virginia bank had been robbed by two men and a woman, right in Harrellsville near the banks of the winding Wiccacon River, three strangers showed up—two men and a woman—and the three of them rented on the spot a big house right in town. The house was partly furnished, and no one saw this trio move anything but themselves into it. The shades were drawn and stayed drawn, and the woman and the men never emerged. No one saw them go in or out or anywhere at all.

Except late of an evening, near dusky dark, one of the three would appear in the side yard, near the magnolia tree, just long enough to get some coals going in a rusty grill, then disappear, and then, twenty minutes later, reappear and stay out just long enough to grill some meat for him- or herself, as it happened to be, and for the other two inside.

Because the light was poor and the viewings were brief and the witnesses few and far between, no one in the tiny hamlet ever got a good, clear look at any of them and so could not have described them for the authorities, had there *been* any authorities to receive descriptions.

This went on for a good while and became a topic of the day in Harrellsville, and whenever locals talked about them, they always referred to them as "the bank robbers" or, as a variant, "the Virginia thieves." Anyone at all would know who was meant by this and, of course, exactly where they were.

Just when it seemed like matters must come to a head, just when everyone thought the thieves must finally be running out of steaks to throw over the coals, just when the law must be on the verge of showing up, surrounding the house and collaring them, another two men and a woman, the *real* Virginia bank robbers, were caught at an A&W root beer stand eight states away.

And then everyone felt guilty and right liable for the constant slandering of the three newcomers, till one of the older heads stopped by the gas station and sounded off to the loafers there, who spread his word, and in so doing helped everyone get a better attitude and rehabilitate both the three new people and themselves as well.

"Here we been suspectin' these new folks, right and left, of robbing the banks up in Virginia and of Lord knows what else goes on in that shut-up house all hours of day and night. Been callin' 'em Virginia thieves *and worse*, when all along—*all along*—it turns out they ain't nothin' but a bunch of *grill nuts*, just like you and me. And that's all there is to it, they're just grill nuts, come to Harrellsville, nothin' else on their minds but to grill."

And so Ann and I became grill nuts too, and within a year or so I started to get a handle on how, with a small grill, to cook chicken, steaks, salmon, hot dogs, rockfish, even pork butts (a longer project than the rest), our grill at that time set in place below our cottage and just twenty feet above the entrance to our field.

As I was usually tending the grill alone for however long it took, I began to step into the moonlight or starlight in the field and, sometimes, to say aloud to the heavens the names of good friends who had passed on—at first just a few, though sooner than I expected many more.

When Hunter got to be in his early teens, he would occasionally come down from the house to keep me company, and I kept my memorial list to myself and we talked about whatever he wished to.

One evening he walked into the field, looking across the west-northwest sky for the Hale-Bopp Comet, and as I was pulling chicken off the grill, he exclaimed, "No way!"

"No way *what*, Hunter?" I asked him, not yet knowing that he was thinking about the recent mass suicide of the Heaven's Gate cult in San Diego, thirty-nine unfortunates who had been promised a spectral, astral getaway associated with the comet. I put the tray of grilled meat down and walked the few steps down into the field.

"No way, Dad," he said, pointing up at the white smudge of moving light in the sky. "No way is there a spaceship up there behind that comet waiting to pick up all those dead people from California."

"No, of course there's not," I said somberly, and we spoke of how sad it was that several dozen perfectly good people had bought into the teachings of such a fabulist as their leader certainly was. And we carried the hot barbequed chicken and the oak-handled grilling fork on up to the house for our family's dinner.

In all these many years of being a Clover Garden grill nut, I have marveled at many a night sky, summer, fall, winter, spring . . . and thought time and again about the mystic spacecraft that never appeared for those willful believers, those doomed Californians back in the spring of 1997. Thought, too, of how many folks in Ann's and my life have gone on, reviewing their lives and saying their names to the night sky.

We may well be the least sparrows of the universe, one way to perceive the astonishing vastness we have long known we were lost in, knowing this even more as the lenses of the James Webb Space Telescope show us daily what long flights await us when we each and all at last fly away home.

In the time we are granted, though, we light a fire now and again, an offering as day turns into night, and make something *talk about good!* for our family and friends, and I thank, as Kipling said, the "living gods" that made us, who let me learn joyfully to become a grill nut at Ann Cary Kindell's gentle hand and direction and who let me stay on as one all these years since, so graciously close to her.

Pool

Here where there is neither hope nor haste
I narrow down my gaze to where I waste
this afternoon away;
on a green field of order, where I wait

for this game's random shifts to bring you back,
high and low, striped and solid balls rotate.
I chalk my cue and call for one more rack . . .
—Henry Taylor, "An Afternoon of Pocket Billiards"

Here at home in the Clover Garden hill country, I once unwrapped a present from Ann and our Cary, a lightweight item in a two-by-three-foot box that turned out to be a miniature pool table replete with three-foot cues and two-inch balls.

And a couple of full-size cubes of blue chalk.

My wife and daughter, knowing my love of the game, intended the gift as humorous, and there was shared mirth aplenty—yet as soon as play and the *sounds of play* began, it became clear how serious and effective this little touchstone was, for I was so easily transported by it back down to Elizabeth City in northeastern North Carolina and my swampy, riverine Pasquotank boyhood:

There, coming from the open upstairs windows of a plain two-story commercial building overlooking a brick-paved side street, Colonial Avenue, as a boy I used to hear the pouring out of loud jolly talk and laughter but most of all the hard clicks of cue balls breaking the racks, and spoken and sometimes shouted encouragements and disappointments, and the lighter clicks of wooden scoring beads, as men I could not see slid them along strung wires above the green felt-covered slate pool tables in that magic room above. A small sign hung by the streetside door, stating simply:

City Billiards, Home of Luther "Wimpy" Lassiter, World Champion, 9-Ball

In the nearby corner movie theater, the Center, my young pals and I often sat, enthralled and forgetting we were only a hundred yards from a swamp river whose waters were on their way from the Great Dismal Swamp down to the sound and the sea, believing instead that we were riding along on horseback as we wove with the cowboys Hopalong Cassidy and Roy Rogers through some saguaro range or that we were stomping or swinging along with Tarzan of the Jungle through equatorial brakes ridden with mamba snakes. We even saw Zsa Zsa Gabor there, in *Queen of Outer Space*, and we knew this short interlude of imaginary intergalactic travel had brought us to our worshipful knees before the most beautiful and powerful woman in the universe.

Yet when we emerged from these diversions, our riverport reality fell heavily upon us, and the sounds of *smack* and *click* kept spilling out from the pool hall on high, and we somehow knew that was where the real men, not boys, went to have their adventures, though all we could do, our ages still in single digits, was to stand on the sidewalk below and listen hard and try and make out what the hoots and hollers and howls, and the cussing, were all about, and what they all really meant.

Years later, at Uncle Joe's home on Greenwood Road, a few hundred yards straight down the Raleigh Road hill below Gimghoul Castle in Chapel Hill, in a large square pine-paneled room stood two grand implements of joy and purpose that guided me through my teenage days: a 1917 player piano and a Brunswick pool table of more recent vintage with a golden-brown felt top. After school, an inspired fellow could get in an hour of honky-tonk piano playing (Ray Charles's "What'd I Say," Floyd Kramer's "Last Date," Allen Toussaint's "Mother-in-Law," as interpreted by Ernie K-Doe) and another good hour of eight ball, even if I were only singing alone and then playing, as well, only against myself. I liked the feel of the ivories, and then I certainly liked the light heft of the cue stick and the faint dusty smell of blue chalk as I squeaked it onto the tip and smacked the cue ball into the rack and heard all that increasingly familiar clack and clatter.

If I could be Ray Charles for a while, then I could also be Wimpy Lassiter for a while too.

And why not?

Why the hell not?

Some of my pals from the Greenwood neighborhood, Tom West and Dave Harrison among them, would also come chalk a cue with me on occasion, so the progression of lonesome though active afternoons would be broken. After a while, about the time we all turned sixteen and could drive (in my case, my uncle gave me the use of a glorious four-cylinder '48 Willys jeep, with no top and only a seagull feather to dip into the flat gas tank beneath the driver's seat to discover how close to empty the vehicle was), we decided to take our skills to town and try out some *real* pool halls, there being one on West Franklin Street and another on West Rosemary Street—the latter said to be owned by Doug Clark, the musician (inspired as a boy by the US Navy's all–African American B-1 Band, which marched majestically day-by-day from its members' segregated housing in Carrboro to the UNC campus) whose perennially popular band the Hot Nuts toured the East Coast by bus on weekends and played fortunes of off-color R&B songs for young college men to alligator to, sinking to floors, trying desperately to impress their dates.

One sunny Saturday morning a quartet of us went into Doug Clark's pool hall and shot for a couple of hours and, as we knew we would, really liked the loud clatter of rack after rack busting apart as ferocious underslung stick action slammed the cue balls, rolling forth into battle. That we were white boys in a Black men's redoubt *seemed* to make little difference, or at least no one showed it if it did. We knew we were no trouble, and we were spending money. We may not have played very well, but we were left alone and had a good morning of it—though as pool shooters we were laughable held up against Doug Clark's veterans.

We got to going to the Brass Rail pool hall over in downtown Durham, its clientele as white and laconic as Doug Clark's was Black and passionate. The men of the Brass Rail were low-energy, cynical, worn down from work in the tobacco factories, older men who drifted in and out, playing two or three rounds of eight ball and drinking two or three longnecks and some of them hacking and spitting the brown juice of their chaws into bright brass spittoons all around the joint.

Our play improved steadily, if slowly, as we visited these emporia, and we played only eight ball, and my comrades found their way to Uncle Joe's piano and pool hall more frequently as well, so the long lone days had given way to days of what we had come to know as pool hall conviviality. Off to ourselves, we could feign in a way that we were up at Doug Clark's or over at the Brass Rail and ape the ways grown men walked slowly around with squinted eyes and assayed the lay of a table as they set up their shots, and the ways they addressed the cue ball, maybe lying well over the table as they did, and slammed a long shot home or maybe just barely kissed a combination shot so the second ball in the combo might lightly curl around an angled cushion corner and fall smartly into the center pocket. We learned that it was not only the shot but also the next shot, and so we learned about the leave.

And that this was all geometry, and psychology, worth knowing.

Nothing, though, had ever elevated the importance of the pursuit of pool and the rooms in which it was pursued to the level it assumed when my father spoke to me one evening and said he wanted to talk seriously to me—I had no idea about what, till he said: "We need to know about where you stand with the draft."

"The *draft*?" I had yet to turn eighteen, and only would during my first term at UNC, a ways off.

"What do you know about it? And I don't mean what you've *heard around the pool hall*—what do you really know?"

Not a long moment, but a keen one. I promised I would follow up, check on whatever I would have to do to register, and so forth. But what was truly meaningful was my father's realistic assumption that I would have, even *should* have, found my way to the pool hall and heard there both the inevitable levity and also serious talk about serious matters and that, also, I might not have yet known how in the midst of animated and, at times, fur-flying talk to tell what of it was real and what was not. My father was letting me know, advising me of the truth in a slant way, that one needed, always, to take the temper of the room, to learn extra-well how to navigate the gathering places, the watering holes and oases of the world, to note which assertions had real grains of truth within them and which ones were as flimsy as those thin wires above the pool tables threading through the wooden scoring beads. And to start to see what danger looked like.

He was telling me that a pool hall was a truly important place, and he was right.

For that first one I ever recalled, City Billiards there in Elizabeth City just a couple of blocks from where my father was born and lived and practiced law and only two miles from where he died, drew many men into its convivial space, many of them rank amateurs, some poseurs with light skills and a trick or two and perhaps a two-bit hustle, and a few truly talented when it came to chalking a cue.

Yet one of them—and *only* one—was the champion of the world.

In time, Jake Mills showed me his two favorite pool halls, Happy's on Cotanche Street in Greenville and Wilbur's on Webb Avenue in Burlington. After school in the 1950s, he and Steve Coley used to play quarter games with the textile mill hands coming off first shift and drifting into Wilbur's straight from work. The cigarette haze hung low below the green shades, and the cry of "Rack!" was in the air, and the balls clicked and clacked, and, like many a youth before them, Jake and Steve picked up pin money in this Alamance County eight-ball haven. When, decades later, Jake and I looked in there late one winter's day, had a cold one, and shot a round, no haze hung and we were just about the only ones in Wilbur's as a gloaming crept over the now shut-down and closed mills at half past five.

Once, at the courthouse square pool hall in neighboring Graham, the bartender serving Jake after a spell began commiserating with him, telling Jake about how his best friend's wife had recently stabbed him in the back with a Bic pen, not really hurting him badly, but still . . .

"Pretty pointed message," Jake said, and the bartender grimaced. "I mean," Jake went on, "she must've thought he wasn't exactly seeing the writing on the wall." At which point the bartender shook his head angrily and walked off.

Sometimes in New York City years ago, my fellow songwriter David Olney (who would have a brilliant career in Nashville) and I found ourselves on the Upper West Side in the big, sixteen-tabled Seventy-Ninth Street Billiards at the northeast corner of Broadway. The hall had a fortune of windows wrapping around its corner, facing west and south, and so had a bright, airy disposition to it, even on a cloudy day. One slow afternoon, the owner, a stocky man about sixty, ambled by as we racked the balls and asked us where we fellows were from. When I said North Carolina, he asked: "Anywhere near Elizabeth City?"

"That's where I grew up—Luther Lassiter's from there!" I went on about City Billiards, about how Lassiter started hanging around there as a boy, got the free use of the tables for keeping the place swept up.

"*Wimpy*—sure. He always comes by here anytime he's in town, runs the table a few times, shows everybody how you do it. Nice guy. The best."

"What about Minnesota Fats?" I asked.

"*Fats*? Aw, he's a loudmouth, a braggart—he's nothing but a hustler."

The New York pool-hall man who had seen it all let that sit a few seconds, nodding at Dave and me both and, just before he walked on through a space that is no more, said with finality: "Wimpy Lassiter's the best nine-ball player I've ever seen. Straight pool too. And on top of that, he's a real gentleman."

Semi-dim places like the Crunkleton in Chapel Hill and the Orange County Social Club in Carrboro featured single tables back away from their front doors, always a nice sight for an eight-ball man or woman, though a single table hardly a pool hall made. Neville's agreeable speakeasy just off Broad Street in Southern Pines with its pair of tables seemed at least halfway there. My son, Hunter, and I were chalking post-Thanksgiving cues not long ago in the OCSC and challenging David and Heidi Perry, and in the ensuing contest across the red-felt table (with red cubes of chalk to match), our energies went betimes vivid, betimes laconic, matching the energy in the small Paris-of-the-Piedmont barroom ("Nice to be channeling the Royal James," David said a time or two).

In former days, women would not have found such welcome in the real pool halls of old. Dave Harrison and I brought our dates into the Brass Rail in

Durham one evening after we had gone to an art film at the Rialto and for that integrative act earned just about the most brazen, hostile glares either of us had ever received. But that age went by the boards sometime as the twentieth century aged and passed on, and pool tables started showing up, along with darts and foosball games, in many a spot that served wine as well as beer. Vic's smoky tavern on Turner Street in Beaufort (where, Ann has told me, a young woman's reputation would be shot should she ever enter) kept its three big, beckoning, green-felt slate tables and changed hands and became the Royal James, smoky no more yet still and all one of the best pool halls in the land and a renowned epicenter of eastern Carolina spirit, welcoming all comers and losing nothing in the bargain.

Channeling the Royal James indeed: nicely put, David Perry.

I have sat in the Royal James, the RJ, on a Thanksgiving-tide afternoon and heard the best of talk from Steve Desper, the late top-tier science educator, about speculative ways to pull nitrogen out of the Neuse River; have read in Barbara Garrity-Blake's Fish Factory of a menhaden fisherman here in the Royal James engaging the captain of the pogy boat upon which they both worked and telling him, movingly, "I know why you fish, Cap'n, 'cause it's in your heart"; have seen a laughing female in a sequined, formfitting camouflage dress pulling the taps behind the bar at a blistering pace one Friday night; have seen another woman polish off male eight-ball opponents on the middle slate table just as fast as they could challenge her—set 'em up, knock 'em back down; and have seen families of every age range taking a few moments off the baking summertime Beaufort streets and cooling out playing the smaller seventy-five-cent tables in the back of the hall.

And over a stretch of thirty-five years I have found the Royal James to be as good a barometer of balance as any around, and far better than most. As much as I have deeply enjoyed concertizing in theaters great and small around the world, even glimpsing seriously at times into corridors of power, and spending so many grand years with our young best and brightest in the halls of academia, I have also learned that a man without time to enter the pool hall for a short while and chalk a cue and go two out of three or three out of five with one's peers is a man missing out on some of life's best essences. For X marks the spot where geometry and conviviality cross and create the billiard parlor, the pool room, and praise be for such a salubrious intersection.

That diminutive pool table, the holiday gift from Ann and Cary all those years ago—with no shadow falling between contemplation and act—immediately became the Royal James Jr. And over many years since its unwrapping, upon its green felt in our red-clay country living room, many a contest of geometry and will has been launched, played with an exacting hilarity, and settled. The relish to rack is the same, the squeak of the chalk the same, and much is spoken and heard around the RJ Jr. pool hall.

And the *smack* and *click* of the white cue and the striped and solid balls are the same as they ever were, just as those clear, sharp convincing sounds were when they leapt out the windows and echoed all over Colonial Avenue and rained down upon us boys there, emanating from Wimpy Lassiter's home court, City Billiards of long ago, where up the same lopsided stairs in the same second-story room near the banks of the Pasquotank River, there is a pool hall yet.

Charlotte Saturday Night

We Red Clay Ramblers were once to perform for a southern conference of recreation directors as the closing event of their Saturday banquet, held in the large hall of one of the main hotels in Charlotte, and so we appeared, loaded in and set up in the late afternoon of an autumn day. A little after eight o'clock, we took the stage and powered out our rousing opening number, the "Saratoga Hornpipe," and a hoedown and "Fisher's Hornpipe," a musical amalgam that we have for years called the "Mile-Long Medley."

At the medley's spirited conclusion, the crowd of about 300 roared.

These were folks who were professionally upbeat—they plied their come-get-in-the-swim wares on cruise ships, in hospitals, at town parks, at camps and schools, and they knew how to insist that *everyone* in any group join in for shuffleboard or singing and dancing, exercise, water ballet or water polo, even thumb-wrestling—anything active that demanded participation, here were gathered the very people who could coax any group's performance onto a higher plane.

They roared, they whistled, they said incomprehensible things and threw their arms up into the air, they drank at will, they had a hard time sitting in their seats and did not want to, so some of them stood and twisted and shook in place, to the hearty cheers of others.

And this response was just to the first musical number of a seventy-five-minute show.

As we played on, the recreation directors, a group fairly evenly made up of women and men, sat energetically dancing with their hands at ten-top, cloth-covered tables, performing for each other no less than we were performing for them. The centerpieces, which we had admired as they were being set out before dinner, were eye-catchingly colorful, crafted to represent the symbols of our state: a green pine bough, a branch of dogwood in flower, some cotton with the bolls cracked open, a few blood-red cardinals for good measure, all of these symbols made of paper.

The recreation directors were an overly friendly audience, singular in their kinetic, extroverted, can't-hold-back way, unused from lifetimes of moving and leading merely to sit back and watch someone else move and lead. Here they had been sitting in Charlotte hotel conference rooms for several days, watching slideshows and listening to industry favorites preach a gospel of good fun and full-throated participation, and now, likely after too-long of a cocktail reception and too much free-flowing wine at dinner, they were primed, to put it rather mildly, and our highly rhythmic string-band music was all the powder keg they needed.

During our fifth or sixth song, from the stage we saw a huge plume of flame rise up at the back of the room.

Someone had set a paper cotton-and-cardinal centerpiece afire.

Most of the room, facing toward the stage, did not see this flame, nor see it settle right down almost as quickly as it erupted, for that back table's folks, having had their playful moment, quickly put it out—as far as they were concerned: no harm done.

And we, the band, played on.

Played on for another scant minute, till just enough smoke rose and found a smoke detector and set off the hotel's fire alarm, a set of noisy, grating buzzers that, following every few buzzes, sounded out a robotic man's recorded voice saying: "Everyone please leave the room now!"

And did they?

What the finest recreation directors of the American South did was quickly look around, decide that there was no fire, thus no danger, and that this accidentally triggered fire alarm was an occasion to co-opt the performance, to play with each other, to sing and to dance!

In seconds, their laughter, their screams and squeals of delight, their joyful leaping out of their seats with attendant chair-banging, all drowned the band out, and we ended our song.

Just then the recreation directors, led by several enthusiastic, hip-shaking contortionists at the front of the room, started clapping and, finding an insouciant rhythm in the fire-alarm man's droning voice, began to sing along:

"Everyone please leave-the-room—NOW!

"Everyone please leave-the-room—NOW!"

These wondrous beings overrode the alarm man's drone and treated him as a rapper and gave him a Latin beat.

And almost at once, they formed a *conga line* and began to dance as they sang.

Every one of them, all of them, gained a hold on the love handles of whoever was hip-shifting just in front of them and shook and shimmied, swayed and swooned through this grand hotel ballroom, the best Charlotte the Queen City could offer them, hundreds of them passionately singing, as if they had known this song all their lives,

"Everyone please leave-the-room—NOW!

"Everyone please leave-the-room—NOW!"

Yet they would *never* leave this room—they were too happy—however this had happened, the southern recreationists were in their element NOW! They were shouting and shambling, their conga line snaking around the big space, and we could see from our vantage point onstage that this show (for which *we* were now the small audience) might just go on forever.

And that was exactly when a fully decked-out squadron of the Charlotte Fire Department entered all the ballroom's side doors, axes held aloft, every one of them suddenly stopped stock-still, standing in awe, astonished, aghast.

"Everyone please leave-the-room—NOW!"

The immediate impulse of the recreation directors, a platoon of them, was to break briefly from the conga line, rush to the firefighters, rush into this line of axes, and to reach out and entreat them to join the inebriates' dance.

"NOW!"

The firemen were not at all amused.

"Exit the room now!" they exhorted.

"Exit *the room* NOW!" sang the recreation directors, as they slowly shimmied for the doors. "*Exit the room* NOW!"

The firefighters seemed tensed to the maximum, as if they all wanted to shake their big red axes seriously at this foolish assembly. We Ramblers dutifully took up the rear, following along down a couple of flights of stairs ("Everyone please leave-the-room—NOW!" echoing loudly in the stairwell) and then on out into a surface hotel parking lot, where the mild chill of fall damped down the dancing and singing and the conga line fell apart into its constituent pieces.

The rec directors looked about, disappointed that no bar awaited them out here in the lot.

After about twenty minutes of milling around desultorily, we all returned to the ballroom—from which the firefighters had removed *every* single one of the paper centerpieces—and we resumed our show. Because the firefighters had moved into the scene and done the party in, a good bit of attrition had set in, as many of the rec directors had headed for the hotel bar, and there was no longer an exuberant spirit in the ballroom. During the applause between a few of the numbers, someone would shout, trying to re-rev up things, "Everyone please . . ." and get slight laughter and mild mitting from the remnant crowd.

For the starch had gone out of the soiree and the evening, the red paper cardinals had flown away for good, and we would wind up our show swiftly—and I would be back home (with a new tale to tell Ann of sophisticated Charlotte), back through the dark Uwharrie Mountains to Clover Garden, just two hours away, by midnight.

A singular evening. Early yet.

Walking Late

About six on a cool late April evening when Ann and I went walking down the lane, we soon heard—from somewhere off in the big piney woods near a pond—both the first thrush singing its flutish, glissing song and the first summer tanager chittering now and again.

These sounds—along with the alternate trilling and thrumming of peepers, tree frogs—spring's woodland markers, were more dear than ever, given the initial pandemic year then just past. We used to note the coming of full spring by the presence of bobwhites and their spring chicks, singing out and all crossing the lane in one straight line, and by the calls of the whip-poor-wills and chuck-will's-widows, but none were to be heard these days—the return of foxes and coming of coyotes had not been kind to such wonderful ground nesters.

Yet to hear the thrush and the tanager within a few moments of each other served as bright cheering notes, for sure.

We often stopped that spring and regarded the fifty-yard drift of bluets, six-feet wide and running like a fairies' road along the east bank of a pond along our evening walks, though on this day we strolled on down the slope to the rill that receives the waters flowing out of that pond, and were we ever rewarded there—by the wild lavender geraniums and the white five-petaled atamasco lilies along the rill.

One evening Ann tied a piece of orange surveyor's tape around a service-berry tree, with a note on the tape: "Do not cut." Called *sarvis* by the early mountaineers and *shadbush* too by our riverine settlers, since its white floral clusters bloomed in April at about the same time shad ran up our eastern rivers to spawn, this small tree had caught Ann's attention because it was the

Atamasco duo

Wild geranium

only one we had ever seen along the lane. After she marked it, we wandered farther, to look in on a pond colony of whirligig beetles that would always go swimming hastily in circles at one's looming approach.

Such were the perennial treasures of these Cape Fear River headwaters: the rill soon flows from the beetles-and-bluets pond into a small south-to-north tributary of Cane Creek, which, after it traverses the old Morrow Millpond and goes over or through the small stone dam, will roll on for another mile or so and deliver its waters to the Haw River.

Some afternoons when we walked we would see a neighbor and his young son fishing the pond from a paddleboat that got no other use but theirs— and not just fishing: *catching*. We had drawn a myriad of tadpoles out of our rain-filled jonboat and repatriated them to this pond, and before long their descendants were frogs, crowding the pond's margins by the thousands.

On many of the evenings when we showed up at the pond and strode to water's edge, the place set up a chorus of *clicking*, a real uproar lasting only about ten to twelve minutes and occurring only when the light lines from the western sun were coming through the pines on the pond's far side at just the right angle. Never, though, could we see the insects that were making all those *clickings*.

Till at last we asked each other: What if they are not bugs, but frogs, making these sounds?

And so they were, we learned: very tiny, thumbnail-sized northern *cricket frogs*, agility champions (they can leap five to six feet) reacting to day's end with a sharp collective percussion that rang out over the pond and off the pines and hickories and oaks that surrounded it.

As we walked back up the way after that April evening of the first thrush and tanager, Ann spied a mayapple in bloom, the modest pale-green flower beneath its pad of a leaf smaller and more subtle than a hellebore. And then moments later we passed a multi-flowered vine of wild Carolina honeysuckle, red blossoms showing off right by the roadside a dozen feet off the forest floor, with fern fiddleheads coiled each like a diminutive chambered nautilus in the ditch banks below, as poet Oliver Wendell Holmes has it, "In gulfs enchanted, where the Siren sings."

We took a census of a small community of very young redbud sprouts growing right where some imminent grading work on the lane would do them in, and then came back two evenings later with shovel and pots and wagon and in short order rescued five of them.

Two we replanted at once near the start of our long drive, where rainwater rolls off the hill and groundwater also seeps out of it, and three young redbuds we carted into the garden and watered them, deferring a decision as to where to put them and watch them grow. For their new home, as they spread up and out, was important, as it would become a sanctuary for members of the church of the redbud, who would often go there in a spirit of praise.

Worship

When our daughter Cary was about nine or ten, she would occasionally stay over with one of the few neighbor children her age out here in the country. These sleepovers usually happened on Saturdays, which more or less obliged Cary to attend church with her host's family.

On one of these Sunday mornings, she told us many years later: "The church was infested with ladybugs!"

The preacher had been droning on till at last he turned to the children in the sanctuary, inviting these little "lambs of God" to come forward and receive blessings, an altar call for the smallest among the congregation. Children were used to such invitations, greatly amusing the adults in the room as they readily shook themselves loose from their parents in the pews and then ran down front to the altar.

All but Cary.

"I wasn't paying any attention," she said years later. "I didn't know anything about this church, what they were doing."

"Cary," a woman had said. "Go!"

But Cary did not go. She was truly oblivious to what was going on with the other children in the chapel.

"Go, go, *go!*" the woman urged her.

Cary could scarcely hear, for she was deeply, hypnotically fascinated with the hordes of ladybugs, the tiny orange beetles strolling along on the back of the pew in front of her, marching up and down the racked hymnals' spines, on the fore edges of their closed texts. Finally, the woman's voice broke through, and Cary had gotten up belatedly and walked forward.

Yet this, and *not* whatever the preacher had said to the lambs once the last of them had taken a place at the altar, was what Cary would remember twenty years later: a whole lot of one of the Lord's favored insects (He created over 100,000 species, British geneticist J. B. S. Haldane said, adding that the Lord had "an inordinate fondness for beetles"), troops of ladybugs patrolling the little country church, looking for aphids to eat, serving the Lord as they did so by also serving the farmers of Clover Garden, protecting their crops, mostly hay and corn and soybeans and milo hereabouts, and with their in-nocuous crawlings lulling this one little girl to watch them so closely and so well that she would not even notice a preacher's altar call, because her eyes were all caught up by the Lord's least creatures right before her and thus by true grace: the endless, tireless workings of Creation itself.

High Summer

At more or less five o'clock on a summer afternoon out here in Clo-ver Garden, some pretty lovely moments are occurring: nuthatches scoot-ing up and down the oaks and hickories, goldfinches at the feeder and at the bath, doves cooing in the near distance and other doves pecking at bird-spilled seed and weaving themselves in and around the always busy squirrels, and cardinals taking their turns on the baffle. Chickadees sneak up onto the deck via a gardenia bush, to flit forth and sip rainwater from a cake pan we had set out, while blue and green dragonflies fly about and sometimes light, and in just a while we will see forest fireflies hovering and blinking just a foot or so above the forest floor—more lightning bugs rising from the tall grass and bats swooping above would make the field at dusk simply come alive.

An eighty-degree summer day is ideal for Ann and me, warm but not roasting in the field, and beneath the forest's canopy around the house, we find the temperature almost ten degrees cooler than that. With a light breeze moving in the field and in the woods, and an overhead fan at medium on the screen porch, the air feels fresh and good, nothing like that near-solid wall of humidity-heavy air off in the huge forests and small towns in eastern Carolina—which prompted, so Douglass Hunt once told me, an old doctor in Gates County to give Doug's uncle, one of the doctor's just-as-old pa-tients, this Depression-era advice about being out in August on the streets of Gatesville: "Drive slow—park often—never get out of second gear."

Being on our screened porch (a five-sided, unfinished octagon) often re-minds me of the hours upon hours in the 1960s when my mother and sisters and I spent evenings sitting with our grandparents on their small screened porch with the big green glider at the Robert Baker Lawson House on East Franklin Street in Chapel Hill, high up the slope above Battle Park, where they lived. This was years before North Carolina ever adopted daylight saving time, so summer sunsets came then by seven-thirty, and several evenings a week we visited with our elders in the summer heat at that big old gingerbread house.

A solitary lime-green light hung above the center of the porch, and all of us seemed bathed in an alien glow, as lightning bugs moved slowly about the porch-screen perimeter and we listened to Grandmama's stories of growing up along the Scuppernong River and how she had loved lilies of the valley since childhood, and mostly to Granddaddy Page's tales of leading construction on the UNC campus in the 1920s, or working on the high, narrow, terrifying Grace Bridge over the Cooper River and staying with Grandmama at the Henry Timrod Inn (imagine a hotel named for a *poet*) in Charleston.

Those were hot, still evenings in town, and we rarely sense them quite that hot out here in the country, but when we do, there always comes a moment that carries me straight back to those lime-green nights and my grandparents' long-gone days that really came to life for them *and* for us during their soft-spoken tones in the heat: Grandmama remembering steamboats calling at Columbia's Scuppernong River wharf, and Granddaddy recalling men poling two-masted schooners up the New River to Tar Landing and to Richlands beyond, to load up with barrels of tar, pitch, and turpentine and then drifting back downriver and sailing down the ocean and up the Cape Fear to the vast wharves and markets at Wilmington.

Would that I could recall every word; fortunately I do recall a delicious lot.

The one phrase I will never forget, though, is what Grandmama would say on the really baking nights, when the temperature would still be over ninety when we arrived to sit with them (for our apartment in Glen Lennox on Chapel Hill's eastern side was even hotter, not air-conditioned at that time) and wait it out. It might take till nine o'clock, and we might have revisited, through their spoken memories, a dozen or more events: Kinston tobacco market tales circa 1900, the US Capitol lawn about 1911 during a major heat wave that drove thousands to that place in the evenings (including my grandparents and their first child).

Pressure in the air around us would lessen and stop pressing all those superheated molecules against each other, and they would move invisibly and back away from us too, and we learned to feel it, really *feel* it, the sultry point at which we could almost anticipate her words, which Ann and I say now when such moments come along, not so much a pronouncement as a benediction, a day-is-done, an *abide-with-me* vespers, when Grandmama would smile, look up, and say: "Mercy, children, the heat has *broken*."

Boatwrights

Early in the fall of 2012, my immediate hilltop neighbor, Dr. Bill Garlick, walked down through the hilltop woods from his place, sat in our cottage living room, and unfurled a set of the Alexandria Seaport's plans for an eleven-and-a-half-foot Bevins sailing skiff, proposing: "How about we build one of these for each of our daughters?"

The beauty of the plans notwithstanding, I had to confess: "Bill, I've been on the water all my life, but I've never built a boat."

"Well, neither have I," he said, "so we're even."

With these precise plans and his just-up-the-hill's full shop with planer, chop saw, and all manner of other tools and clamps, Bill may not have been exactly a rack-of-eye boatbuilder, yet he was still an old salt, having grown up in Baltimore and in Buxton, North Carolina, right on the edge of the high wild dunes and swamps of the thousand-acre Buxton Woods, and more recently boating and fishing from his Marshallberg Down East fish camp A-frame (with a clear view of Cape Lookout Light), all around Core Sound and Cape Lookout too.

So the Sunday after Thanksgiving, in Bill's shop beneath the oaks, wood-stove cranking, we took the first steps, scarfing several four-by-eight sheets of marine plywood together for decking and sides, and we were off. With both of us working full-time, our sessions were few and far between, though, and months passed into years, and yet we kept at it, now the transom, now the single rib, now the gunnels.

We worked through the many hours of what the plans insightfully called "soulless sanding."

We took great pride in our centerboard trunks.

On the shop radio, we loved listening to Louis Jordan's jump blues and Jimmy Reed's sharp harmonica numbers on NC Central's lively WNCU 8-Track Flashback show of a Saturday afternoon, to Bob Marley's "One Foundation" and King Sunny Adé's "Let Them Say" on the reggae and Afro-Pop Worldwide shows on Sundays.

More than once, when one or the other of us sustained a cut or got a splinter, Bill the medic with Land Down Under, South Seas experience would say: "Need an Australian Band-Aid," a small piece of paper towel applied with electrical tape. Enough time did pass with us a-building, though, to the point that champion boatbuilder Jimmy Amspacher of Marshallberg Down East in Carteret County—he who many times now had knocked a sixteen-foot Core Sound skiff together over a January weekend in the lobby of Asheville's Grove Park Inn—asked me: "You ever going to sail that boat of yours, or is it just going to be a planter?"

From Bill's waterside place in Marshallberg, with Ann's help one July afternoon in 2016, we launched the first of the two boats, painted white just like another legendary boatbuilder, James Allen Rose, said all Core Sound

Launching skiff in Marshallberg

craft should be, once recalling for me the boats of his boyhood: "You'd see 'em sailing down the sound, and if they were coming through a fog, they looked just like a bunch of *ghosts*."

The southwest wind carried us a half mile out that day in a heartbeat, Bill holding the sail's sheet and I the tiller—we were well beyond the old Confederate hole, the east end of Brown's Island where the Rebels had once had a fort to guard against Union vessels approaching Beaufort or Fort Macon from Core Sound above, both fort and the sandy ground it had sat upon long since eroded away and sunk into the sound.

Much as I enjoyed piloting, I let us down, trying to return with way too long a beam reach when I should have been dutifully tacking, and as we neared land again we were most of half a mile downwind of our embarkation point and needed to paddle and pull to get the craft back to where we could take out.

Guardian

Still and all, the little white skiff we had built way upstate in Bill's Clover Garden shop proved worthy before a moderate breeze, stable and not a bit tippy as we moved within her, tight and no leaks whatsoever, leaving us two old salts on the inaugural sail to make good headway and to get just as wet as we wished, and no wetter.

The Road to Jack's

Half of the ten-mile ride through the country from our place down to Jack Herrick's home under the big oaks near Mann's Chapel—our Red Clay Ramblers headquarters—covers Crawford Dairy Road, a long flat stretch on its upper end, yielding to rolling hills on its lower, named for its main feature: a Holstein dairy farm not quite midway from the flashing light on the Old Greensboro Road on the north end to decades-old Frosty's (now Aidan's) trading post at its south.

I have driven this road hundreds of times, at all hours of day and night, because over the years Rambler rehearsals have often gone past midnight and returns from our touring treks might occur at dawn, noon, or midnight, and, whatever the hour, there is always much to see on this classic Carolina Piedmont two-lane blacktop, so much worthy of estimation.

Once, coming back home to Clover Garden after a picking session, as I passed Crawford Dairy (that family five generations now on the land) I came upon a couple of dairy cows that had stepped through the fence and were now trying to find their way back into the pasture from the roadside. I called Howard Crawford when I reached home, and after seventy-five rings or so, he answered sleepily, heard my report, and, presumably, repatriated his cows to the field.

Another time, about midnight just a couple hundred yards south of John Crawford's auto body shop, I rounded a curve only to see fifteen or twenty dairy cows going slowly north in the southbound lane, and, after passing them oh-so-slowly myself on their right, this being only a scant mile from the well-traveled Old Greensboro Road, rather than let the phone ring on at Crawford Dairy, instead I rang 911 immediately and got word to the dispatcher that a dairy herd was steadily approaching the flashing light intersection and that both Highway Patrol and animal control were called for—*at once*—at that remote spot, lest unfortunate eventualities might soon occur.

John Crawford, a stocky, good-humored man, and I have been friends for several decades now. Given his innate skills with cars and sheet metal ("There's no *book* for body work!" he says), he has helped many Clover Garden folk over the years, me for certain in one of the family's more unusual efforts, to wit: my son, Hunter, perhaps a month after obtaining his driver's license in high school, while out driving our jeep, reached up to adjust the rearview mirror and looked back down again just in time to see the jeep's front end plow into a late-model Lincoln Continental Town Car's rear end, where, as design would have it, *all* its electrical circuitry was housed.

One of the better auto insurers took care of all this, paying $10,000 to repair the Lincoln while totaling the jeep. Hunter and I decided that we, together, could trade out the jeep's hood and front side panel and bring the maroon vehicle back, and, for the cause, fellow fisherman Shannon Hallman down on Lystra Church Road gave us his long-defunct, same-year jeep (a deeper maroon model, which had sat in his barn for twenty years or more) for parts.

John Crawford loaned me a set of Torx wrenches and wished us the best of luck, adding in some leavening advice and caution, reminding us: "There's no book."

We took the bent pieces off our jeep, undid the perfectly good replacements from Shannon's vehicle, found that in the heat of that summer, under threat of wasps and hornets, we simply could not get much further, so then took the stripped-down jeep, with the replacement hood and side panel, back over to John Crawford, who put it all back together and had us fixed up in just a few days' time.

One day John asked me if I had ever happened to notice a little house at the corner of Wildcat Creek and Old Greensboro Road, one that used to be a gas station and, though long decommissioned, still had a twenty-six-foot concrete pad surrounded and covered by golden-tan Chapel Hill gravel out front. I said yes, so without further ado John spun me the yarn of when that was an active filling station and he was sixteen. After filling up his muscle car, he peeled out and laid rubber across the entire length of that pad and went roaring off into the Bingham Township night.

The next time John stopped in there, a week or so later, the older man running the place said, "Here, John," handing him a bucket, some sort of solvent, and a brush and sponge, saying, "Now you go out there and clean every bit of that rubber you laid down last week off my concrete."

"But—"

"And if you *don't*, first thing, you'll never buy gas here again, *and* second thing, I'll use that quarter I been saving that it'll cost me to call your daddy long distance and let him know what a wild-ass hot dog his son really is. How about getting to work?"

So John Crawford in short order got to work.

South past Crawford Dairy itself, where for years the Crawfords have sold eggs from a basket set outside their milking parlor just a few feet from the edge of the road (eggs from their hens now being on sale at Bravo's Market out on NC 54, sister enterprise to the Mexican Fiesta Grill across the highway at White Cross, welcome additions as a Hispanic presence increases

Big fields on road to Jack's

Nightshade in big fields

here, as in all across North Carolina), almost a mile of great fields lay out ahead, open and lovely green with wheat during the wintertime, full of feed corn on one side in the summer and fall, soybeans on the other. Across these fields, on the way to rehearsal once, I saw the largest and most brilliant sunset clouds in the distance beyond, clouds that had followed a thunderstorm and put the storm to shame with their huge, recuperative glory.

When we have had several days of rain, anyone driving this way can see down through a big draw on the west side of Crawford Dairy Road and catch a glimpse of the Haw River running high at flood stage, though the river does not show itself there at any other time—only when it is cresting. Then the road falls away, down to Collins Creek, near where the foundations of a nineteenth-century grinding mill on this creek still stand, the creek waters rushing past and through those ruins.

Collins Creek and a side road three-quarters of a mile past it are both bound for the Haw River near Chicken Bridge, site of the legendary 1950s chicken-truck wreck that left flocks of feral poultry roaming the riverside woods for months and gave the span its abidingly popular name. For many a year the simple directions for Chapel Hillians of a certain age (during the era of renting cheap old farmhouses way the hell out of town and throwing bedsprings barbeques and budget Boone's Farm apple wine–fueled parties) on where to find their country compatriots down across the Haw began with the words: "Go to Frosty's Trading Post, turn right, go two miles to the Big Rock, turn left, and cross Chicken Bridge!"

And some who were more into a certain naturist vein in that time and population, and clearly in a certain know, might modify the phrase: "Go to Frosty's, take a right, go two miles, turn left at the Big Rock *just past Pete Thorn's sauna on the right (the sign says 'Mustard Seed Farm')*, and cross Chicken Bridge!"

Just a little ways over Chicken Bridge, where my dear artist-lawyer sister, Sherri, and I used to sit on the rocks some Fridays with a cold one and watch the river flow, and then a mile south on Old NC 87, a green lane sign still says *Rock Rest Rd*. Here at his home, Rock Rest, jurist Edward Jones took in a fellow Irish American, the orphaned Johnston Blakeley, as his ward, and Blakeley, young and impoverished by a fire that destroyed his inherited warehouse wealth in Wilmington, finished his several years as an honor student (and president of the Philanthropic Society) at the new University of North Carolina and joined the US Navy.

As a mariner, Johnston Blakeley took part in the Barbary Coast campaign, and later, in the War of 1812, he led his sloop *Wasp* in an astonishing string of raiding successes against the British on their own home waters, including the English Channel itself. After these historic victories, on October 9, 1814, *Wasp* spoke *Adonis*, a Swedish brig, near the Azores, and after that was never seen nor heard from again.

Yet Commander Blakeley's acute damage to British shipping had opened the way for a rain of American privateers in action all around Britain and beyond that autumn, and when Captain Tom Boyle of the raider *Chasseur* of Baltimore proclaimed to Lloyd's of London (and therefore to the British Admiralty) that the United States had now placed the entire British Isles under blockade, the tide had clearly turned—the War of 1812 was all but over, and the intense offensive naval strategy of UNC's and Chatham County's Johnston Blakeley had carried the day, though North Carolina's war hero did not live to see it and will be forever mourned: *Lost at sea.*

One Fourth of July many years ago, an inimitable pair of artistic, local fireworks makers, blacksmith Paul Gove of Vulcan's Forge, Hillsborough, and the jack-of-all-trades redhead Jim Walker, staged an astonishing display down at Frosty's Trading Post, blasting off canisters that produced helices of mauve and ochre and all manner of pinks and ceruleans cascading down. Paul and Jim's show starred colors and patterns no one had ever seen before in standard-fare municipal bright white and red *ka-boom* fireworks, as theirs were pastels ribboning down and around each other across the night sky. Some 2,000 people, many of them families with children, stood and talked and watched with awe, and there was no security force, no police whatsoever—the largest crowd I was ever in that regulated itself with skill, good humor, kindness, and enthusiasm for the art form Paul and Jim were giving freely to the community.

One can only hope those two felt the true gratitude of their neighbors that warm festive evening.

On an alternate night near this same spot, just after New Year's of 1986–87, video editor and cool-jazz bassist Joe DeLuca and I recut our *King Mackerel & The Blues Are Running* musical's second-act film footage—a collage of news and weather images of 1950s and '60s hurricanes projected during a song-cycle of storm and recovery in the show—at a studio up on Terrell's Mountain. The stars were extraordinarily dazzling that frigid night, and after we were done we drove the several miles down the winding, deer-thick road to Frosty's, where the sky was open and, after parking and getting out of our cars, we could really get an eyeful of the vast, bright wintry heavens.

We had a pair of celebratory beers in a little blue cooler that we set aside down on the ground and then went strolling about an empty roadside area of thirty yards' length, picking out constellations, when here suddenly came a Chatham County sheriff's squad car with a pair of deputies to check on Frosty's door locks. As their car lights swept around and shone right on us, they got out of their squad car, quickly pulled on Frosty's front door, and then walked over to visit us, as Joe and I agreed quickly and sotto voce that the little blue cooler, now some distance from us, was no longer ours. We had no issue with the law, nor did we wish any—there may have been some regulation about beer on a county road right-of-way. Best not to tempt fate.

"Evening, gentlemen," one deputy said. "What are you all doing out here?"

"Just watching the stars," we said.

"Un hunh, watching the stars, un hunh," he said, and after shining his flashlight around, he asked: "That cooler over there, that yours?"

"No sir," Joe said, looking up toward Orion and his neighbors.

"Not yours?" he said. "Well, whose is it?"

"Somebody must've left it," I said.

"Right," he said. "But you don't know anything about it?"

"We're just here for the stars," Joe said, with the decorous serenity we all knew him by.

"Well, all right," said the deputy, edgily. "How 'bout showin' me some stars? Like the North Star."

I pointed out Polaris, saying with an ill-advised cheekiness that it would be a lot easier to see if their squad car lights were not so bright, dimming our night vision.

The deputy cared little for the stars and said again, "You sure you don't know anything about that cooler."

"The stars are why I'm here," Joe said, with his same eternal calm.

"Well," the deputy, glaring at us, said to his partner, "let's go. Best grab that cooler, Bud . . . *for evidence.*"

They backed out very slowly, letting their bright lights shine upon us for half a minute . . . while they had us lit up, Joe and I were pointing randomly up at the brilliant sky, and Joe whispered: "I'm trying real hard not to laugh."

Then they put the squad car into forward and turned away, on down Jones Ferry Road toward the Haw River and Bynum. As soon as the deputies' taillights disappeared, we fell into a state of starlit giddiness for five minutes at least, before saying good night and driving off in our different directions, Joe to Carrboro, I back up Crawford Dairy Road to Clover Garden.

For we both knew that in just a few days *King Mackerel* would be rocking the boards in New York City, at theatrical restaurateur Steve Olsen's West Bank Cafe's Off-Off-Broadway stage (now the Laurie Beechman Theater), the first of many happy and successful times we would run there.

So all was well at Frosty's that night—the stars would await our return, and Joe DeLuca and I would continue our celebration at a later date, without deputies, merely a pleasure deferred down along the road to Jack's house.

Maple View

Many years back, where Dairyland Road came into eastern Bingham Township miles north of Clover Garden, contoured cornfields fell away to the west where a vineyard now grows, and a great hill rose up beyond them a couple miles west of the Calvander crossroads, presenting an old white farmhouse in the maple grove like an agrarian jewel, the dairy herd of Holstein-Friesians before it, the milking parlor out back.

A prominent Hillsborough attorney once told me that when he was but sixteen, living in the Orange Grove community decades ago, dairyman Bob Nutter arrived from Maine at Maple View Farm, he and his family and their herd in trucks, to take his first possession of the farm in the middle of the night.

The man who had sold Maple View to Nutter had pledged there would be a barn full of hay upon his arrival, but Nutter found the barn empty, forcing the near-desperate man to go about the farming neighborhood before first light, seeking help from other Bingham Township dairymen. It was a rude entrance for Nutter, a truly progressive farmer, but his new farm neighbors turned it around and quickly so—the future lawyer told me of going with his father, filling many a truck with bales of hay that night and getting those truckloads over to Maple View just in time for Nutter's dawn feeding and milking.

I used to drive my '48 Willys jeep out that way, heading for Chestnut Ridge, a chapel and church camp well past Orange Grove, about ten miles farther west, always slowing on the Maple View hilltop curve with the long, quarter-mile gaze toward the Nutter home (a graceful, calming view, as I would often think back on it during years living in New York City, in crowds, on the screeching subterranean trains), slowing again and sometimes stopping just before Orange Grove itself to call cows over to a fence line, just to see if I could.

Years ago at Chestnut Ridge we sang Del Shannon's "Runaway," though not a Methodist one among us could have conceived of being a young transient, a vagrant, homeless, any more than we could really identify well with Jack and his fed-up-and-had-it woman in Ray Charles's "Hit the Road Jack," though the Beatles' "A Taste of Honey" was the sensual, aching number that suited our young moments there perhaps all too well. We ate sloppy joes, talked about Jesus and civil rights and increasingly the war, swam in the sixty-acre lake, canoed back into its swampy-wood tributaries, of course sang "Kumbaya" earnestly fireside at full dark, then slunk away earlier than we might have wished to our campsites: wooden platforms three feet off the ground, four single-bed pallets for sleeping bags within each and a canvas Conestoga wagon rig for a roof over each platform. Tree frogs and crickets sang out in dense, pulsing roars, a deafening chorus, the deep, inspired music of a spring Carolina night, as most everyone on the boys' side soon drifted off to sleep, dreaming of some young woman back in town or, better yet, perhaps someone just over on the far side of the camp, protocols placing women a healthy half a mile away, and those few rare young men who snuck out of their quarters did so to little avail, wandering aimlessly in dense woods till circling back to the wagons, and those who were caught out predawn would later be publicly judged "Such a disappointment to us" by the camp leaders. A few times In the fall we were piled into the back of a big farm truck for an hour-long Saturday night hayride, a semi-innocent form of bundling our elders must have knowingly given us, a lesson in yearning toward a particular future that never quite arrived.

And then these pastoral weekends ended, almost before they had even begun, of course all too quickly and way before they had ever had a chance to get in any way what we would later come to call *cranked up*. Sometimes, on Sundays before we left, we would have gone to morning services up at Chestnut Ridge Church, a small brick chapel that might have seated eighty or a hundred. Years later I would still remember one brutally hot summer morning there and a young mother with two small sons, the older of whom started grinding his back against the pew and rolling over in it, liturgically bleating, "I'm hot, Mama, I'm hot, I'm *so* hot!" and then, after five minutes' of her working to get him fully shushed, the younger boy followed the older with his own mantra, "I gotta pee, Mama, I got to, I got to, I got to pee *sooo* bad," her taking him away, returning only to find the hot brother yowling and rolling in the heat again, at which point she gave up and exited left with her undone children as we laughed, while an unctuous young preacher, most likely in his first charge, tried vainly to pretend that none of this was happening, knowing in his heart (we could just tell) that his rhetorical gifts, his flights of fancy speech of inspiration and admonition, his reading of God's word as handed down by the lyricists of King James's court, all were useless in the company of this unworthy lot, these heathens, though he brought Matthew 7:6 to bear and tried: *Do not give what is holy to the dogs; nor cast your pearls before swine, lest they trample them under their feet, and turn and tear you in pieces.*

Poor reverend: he must have been praying to be lifted out of this rude country, such a hard way and place to serve the Lord, and to be dropped kindly into a vineyard more bountiful, gracious, and appreciative and deserving of his gifts, where no babes were whining and no lusty youths were sitting before him yet hearing him not as they fell, invisibly, to envisioning thin spiderwebs of sin: *Sunday morning going down . . . down . . . down . . .*

Back to town in the Sunday afternoons: no spirited Friday expectancy now, no rising feelings while passing Maple View, approaching now from the west, town-ward, and yet there were real residual passions left over from those retreats, and they would soon, or in time, settle where they may among us young communards.

In more recent times, my son, Hunter, asked me why they were building a gas station at the top of the Maple View hill, from whence came the evening view. Though the framing going up was that of a building about service-station size, I assured him that there was no way the Nutters would do such a thing—they had already put the entire farm under an agricultural conservation easement; Maple View would be a farm of some sort in perpetuity.

When I later told Hunter I had heard that the Nutters, who were by then operating a popular, sustainable, bottled-milk commercial dairy, were now planning an ice-cream parlor for that new building, he scoffed and said, "This far from town, no way! Never make it!"

I reminded him of how good their milk was, how well thought of the Nutter family was, and how incredible the afternoon and sunset views from the parlor's front porch would be, but still he gave the prospective enterprise no chance at all.

Months later, Bingham Township and our entire county seemed to have become aware at the very moment Maple View Farm Ice Cream opened its doors. When I stopped there one afternoon—cars and bicycles overflowing the lot and out onto the roadside—to get into a long line for a cone of peach ice cream, I spied Hunter and half a dozen of his fellow Chapel Hill High School seniors sitting in a line of rocking chairs, moving fore and aft slowly, licking away on cones, facing west, soaking it all up as if that evening sun were setting just for them and giving them this day their very own once-in-a-lifetime, ever-lingering, never-to-be-forgotten, million-dollar *Maple View*.

Water Haul

One Saturday we met up near Saxapahaw—Jake Mills, Steve Coley, UNC's tall, affable writing center director Hank Powell, and I—to go dove hunting somewhere in the geo-acronymic UCLA territory (Upper Chatham, Lower Alamance). We had the landowner's permission to hunt, and Jake and Steve's former boss from Burlington's Oak Grove Cafe, Frank "Bear" Webster, was already there, awaiting us near an enormous microwave relay tower that stood high over hundreds of acres of cut corn.

"I don't see much in the way of doves," Bear said, "but there ain't no shortage of buzzards."

Scores of black vultures rested all over the crosspieces of the tower. And Bear was right about doves, too—they were just not flying, and would not be, and not a one of us had fired a single shot that long, hot afternoon.

After we called it a day, I rode with Bear on the Football Road (what the Burlingtonians and Greensborians called the Old Greensboro Road, from the decades when it was the only route from Guilford and Alamance Counties down to Chapel Hill for the Tar Heel games in Kenan Stadium) when, coming around a bend just north of Lindley Mills, a quail jumped up from the ditch and Bear's right headlight knocked it down onto the roadside.

Bear slowed at once, saying, "Kilt a pottridge," turned around, and went back to fetch it and put it into his trunk, the only bird taken that day.

We wound up gathering to review the day's hunt at a small tavern out on the western edge of Saxapahaw. I believe Jake bought us a round and toasted desultorily: "Well, here's to another damn water haul."

In addition to purveying the standard brands (Bud, Schlitz, and PBR) and nothing else, the tavern owner made a locally celebrated chowchow and sold it over the bar in one-quart Mason jars, which were stacked on display in three ranked lines, bespeaking the three levels of heat the owner put to the mash in the making: Regular, Hot, and Double H. (Jake said Double H tasted great and you would really souge down on it, but it was so hot "It'll make you feel like you're gonna die and afraid you won't!")

When I requested a jar, the owner asked me only, "Sure you up to it?" My companions moaned mockingly when I left with a jar of Double H, yet Jake in issuing his warning had not been kidding.

For the concoction made a feast of finely chopped multivariate peppers and cabbage and some secret small vegetables too, topping off any sort of down-home supper with style and grace (red beans and rice never had it so good), and then when its vinegar finish came in hot and got hotter, astonishing and unremitting with its powers, well, it was Katy bar the door and Lord have mercy on the mariner.

Heat?!

I mean. An entire year passed before I got through the whole jar.

Saxapahaw

The first time I saw the Haw River mill and hill village of Saxapahaw I was fourteen, and Sellers Manufacturing spinning mill, owned by US senator B. Everett Jordan and his family, was humming—the huge, multi-story brick building high above the broad, rocky brown-water stream and the great dye plant farther up the hill that received the mill's yarns and colored them to please the world. My compatriot Colin Stewart and I were on a bicycling day trip from Chapel Hill: aiming to cross the Haw River again (having crossed once already at Union Bridge), dammed here in Saxapahaw at the head of the river's navigation. A late nineteenth-century black-and-white photograph I have since come across shows a couple of men and a boy in an overladen open work boat—a bateau—with several bales of cotton and a cow at the river's edge. Colin and I also planned to recross the Haw miles to the south at Chicken Bridge. But we did not really know the lay of that land and so overshot the mark by many miles and at last got back across at Bynum instead, heading north toward home as darkness fell upon us just above the bridge, my mother soon coming to rescue us.

Years later, once I had moved into the Schopler cabin beside Cane Creek, which fed the Haw downstream of Saxapahaw, several times I walked the path on the creek's slick red-clay banks down below Austin's Quarter. And I kept a PO box in the very small hillside Saxapahaw post office there for years, the closest one to the cabin and the one where there was *never* a line.

One afternoon, trying to make the 4:30 p.m. dispatch, I stood at the window while the postmistress weighed and stamped my packages, looking past her and wondering why the mailroom behind her sounded the way it did.

"Have pigeons moved into your post office?" I asked, and she laughed.

"That's just the Burnham row-llas," she said, or seemed to say. "Back there in them boxes."

"The what?!"

"The *Bir-ming-ham rol-lers*," she said more slowly.

"And what are they?" I said.

"Trick pigeons, you know, they spin, they roll when they dive. Fellow here raises 'em, ships 'em out all over creation."

"Oh. New to me," I said.

"Yeah," she said. "Does sound kinda funny in here when there's a box or two of 'em waiting to go out."

Modern times in Saxapahaw: the Jordans sold the mill to Dixie Yarns, which ran it briefly and closed it down in 1994. Then the Jordans bought it all back, with Mac Jordan (who as an NC State architecture student

Founder Ross Flynn at the counter, Left Bank Butchery, Saxapahaw

had studied repurposing just such a property) now overseeing a real-world redevelopment of the old mill as the center of a vigorous village. A visionary couple, Heather and Tom LaGarde, got highly involved in this renewal, set up a Saturday farmers' market (where most buyers encountered meat from lean hogs from Ossabaw Island, Georgia, for the first time, thanks to Eliza MacLean of Cane Creek Farm) and a free concert series from late spring to early fall, and converted the big empty dyeing plant into a serious concert venue—the Haw River Ballroom—where one might see and hear on a given night Gillian Welch and David Rawlings, or Marti Jones and Don Dixon, or the Drive-By Truckers, or former students from my first songwriting class at Carolina: the fine young folk band Mipso and their sounds (which the inventive songwriter and multi-instrumentalist Andrew Marlin called "dark holler pop"). Down the hill in an old riverside gym, some of the largest, strangest theatrical birds, critters, and peoples' heads came into being by the novel workings of Paperhand Puppet Intervention.

Suddenly, so it seemed, the old mill village had become a destination for bicyclists, homeopathic therapy seekers, organic meat and produce growers and consumers, all in all a twenty-first-century version of what the 1970s back-to-the-landers, the "Country Left" of that day, had dreamed and hoped for yet for the most part could never achieve. The General Store, near the top of the hill with Saxaco fuel pumps outside, acquired a kitchen with some "cheffy-ness" about it, compelling celebrated novelist Daniel Wallace (of *Big Fish* and *This Isn't Going to End Well* renown) to call Saxapahaw the home of North Carolina's only five-star gas station. At the other end of the building, past the popular grass-fed meats of Ross Flynn's Left Bank Butchery, above a coffee shop oft haunted by poet Gaby Calvocoressi (*Rocket Fantastic*) and two stories above the fanciful Haw River Brewery, the funky and convivial Eddy bistro gave patrons both local brews and a way-up-high, panoramic view of the Haw River's rocky rapids down below.

Lawyer Ted Teague, who has lived here for most of a decade and who represents a number of its entrepreneurs, says: "I feel lucky every day that I wake up in Saxapahaw and see folks coming from far and wide to enjoy what's in my backyard. For me, it has everything I want and nothing I don't. Most of all, I love the community of like-minded people who gravitate here, a big-hearted group, a merry band of visionaries who care about community and place and are constantly working to keep it special."

The mill village had simply reinvented itself during the late twentieth and early twenty-first centuries. The post office still maintained half-day hours, even though every postal worker I had ever met there would shake his or her head at some point and declare that the PO might not last that much longer. And though I had not kept a box there for many years, I still have the intuitive habit of racing over to get something out in that last Saxapahavian dispatch.

Because there was a river involved, though, some things have not changed, cannot change.

Lake Saxapahaw above the dam spreads out broadly and more than a little wild, with only a bit of lakeside housing and plenty of big sycamores and willow bush thickets along its shores and upon its islands, and Ann and I, out floating the lake from time to time, have often seen far more blue herons than any boater might expect on any given afternoon—the great birds love these Piedmont waters.

When massive Hurricane Fran thoroughly surprised an already drenched central North Carolina, flash-flooding our territory in the late summer of 1996, when great oaks and pines lay right over like sea oats in a heavy gale, she turned so much water loose in the upper Haw basin that Saxapahaw's riverside Methodist church (on the *Right* Bank) flooded, I heard it told, all the way to right up under its two-story eaves.

Nowadays, children swing and play on a big wooden whale out on the island park between the twin Buddy Collins Bridges over the Haw, and lovers stroll beneath great trees along the riverbank trail running just a few feet above the water at the river's normal flow.

Over the last decade, the man who has so vigorously developed this and other Alamance County trails—Brian Baker, another visionary, now the assistant county manager—has gotten twenty of Alamance's thirty-five miles of Haw riverside into the county trails system. His first trail along the river (which has more fall than any other in the Piedmont) was cut under Baker's leadership, he has said, "by prisoners with sharp implements": brush axes. Baker has spent enormous energy settling riverine property owners' fears of hikers lighting fires on their lands or coming to rob them or bothering their animals—"The legend of cow tipping," he says, "is *strong*."

An angled stone fish weir stands out well in the shallows just off the Haw River island not far below the Collins Bridges, reminding us of earlier settlers, earlier times, of the native Sissipahaw, who left their name on this valley and cultivated its Old Fields, and their unknown, unnamed ancestors, lost peoples of long-lost millennia who nonetheless had once fished this river and in their own time had known its waters well.

Devil's Tramping Ground

Six of us boys—all fourteen, all with Sturmey-Archer three-speed bicycles—lit out from Chapel Hill midmorning one April Saturday in 1963. The rolling voyageurs: Colin Stewart, Clyde Milner, Mark Smith, Carl Lewis, Steve Adams, and I. Having written to and gained permission from the Chatham County pony rancher who owned the mythical Harper's Crossroads property in Bear Creek—where no human (we had all read) had ever been able to spend an entire night due to Beelzebub's nocturnal rambles—we were bound to make the forty-mile ride to go camping *right on* the Devil's Tramping Ground.

We would do it—Lucifer could not take all six of us. Strength in numbers.

Our southwesterly route wound bizarrely across southern Orange County and central Chatham County; our bicycles had packs and tents and tent poles strapped to them, and we stopped often to rest and drink water. Once we pulled over to inspect a doorless, windowless abandoned home full of old

Fish weir, Haw River at Saxapahaw

newspapers, broken glass, a few pieces of bent silverware—a curiosity of a quarter hour to us, who were too young to comprehend fully what an evidence of heartbreak and loss we were wandering through.

About four o'clock that afternoon, we reached Siler City in western Chatham, then and for a long time yet to come a chicken processing and livestock auctioning town, in recent years a community far more diverse than it long had been, due to recent Hispanic migration. (Decades later, my son, Hunter, would one day teach English as a Second Language here. And nowadays the little town awaits a major computer-chip wafer-making installation.)

"I'll be right back," I shouted to my comrades. I had spotted the town's police station and had made a blood-pledge to my mother that yes, I would inform the local constabulary about our camping trek so they would know to keep an eye on us; I had to keep my promise before moving on.

Two patrolmen were talking lazily when I came through the door and announced myself and told them who we were and where we were bound.

"So what?" one said.

"Yeah," said the other, "what'd you 'spect us to do about it?"

Their reaction threw me.

"I don't know," I said. "I was just supposed to let you know."

"Okay, now we know."

"Who put you up to this?"

"My mother," I said.

"Okay," the first patrolman said. "I think we got it. Now we know you're out there, you can go on."

I was flummoxed; they had not even said good luck to me on my way out the door. My compatriots had kept going, from the look of it, and I took off to catch up with them, only realizing after speeding down a long, steep hill that the sun was behind me, when it should have been on my right.

In a growing panic I pushed my bike back up that hill, went through the middle of town, passing the police station while hoping the two men inside did not see me, and found the right road, the one going due south to Harper's Crossroads. I had only been inside with the patrolmen a few moments, but the wrong direction and the big hill had cost me—I might now be as much as fifteen minutes behind the rest, who for reasons unbeknownst to me had all pedaled away while I checked in with the police.

Now I pedaled as strongly as I possibly could, expecting to see my five comrades as I rounded each curve, crested each hill. But nothing. Before long I realized that we had only an hour or hour and a half of daylight left, and most of ten miles yet to go. What would I do if I did not find the group or failed to reach the Devil's Tramping Ground? I was not one of the riders hauling one of the two tents—where would I sleep? This was a very fresh situation, for which I had no experience or guidance. My only hope was to try and figure out what Huck Finn would do, and when the thought came back that, at worst, I might find a barn and some hay to sleep on, I felt better.

Yet only a very little bit better.

The day advanced, the sun still above the trees, though not by much. Another couple of panic-driven cycling miles, oak and pine forests on both sides, now and again farmhouses and pastures.

And barns.

Then I came sluggishly over a hilltop and saw the quintet, all standing by their wheels no more than a quarter of a mile away, then mounting them and all rolling on again. I shouted and shouted, called till I was hoarse, and finally one of them heard and turned, and they all stopped and I at last caught up with them.

"What happened to you?"

"Where the hell were you?"

"You were right there, and then you were gone!"

"We just climbed a fire tower up this dirt road to see if we could see you."

So winded was I that I could barely choke out my side of the story. Had they not stopped and tried the fire tower gambit, I surely would not have reached them.

Light was failing, and so, reunited, we headed on south in the dusky dark, another five miles till Harper's Crossroads and full dark and a second check-in, this one at the pony farm not far from the Devil's Tramping Ground.

The short, portly pony man answered his door and invited us into his knotty-pine-paneled den, where he had been watching the rhinestone cowhand Porter Wagoner's country music program. "I like this show," he admitted, just before Porter and the band opened up with a medicine-show-styled ad: "If your snuff's too strong, it's wrong, try Tuberose, mild Tuberose . . ."

"I 'bout give up on you boys, time it's gotten to be," he said.

"We just got away a bit late," one of the others said, a grace for me.

Emboldened, I immediately asked him: "So we'll be the first ones to ever spend the whole night at the Devil's Tramping Ground, right?"

The pony farmer gave me a quizzical stare, held it a few seconds, and said, "Who told you that?"

"That's what all the books say—nobody ever has."

"Well, that may be," he replied. "But there's already been a few."

He sat in an easy chair as we stood, all shoulders lowered by this worse-than-disappointing news. In the background, Porter Wagoner and his boys were launching into a laxative ad, singing desperately: "Black Draught makes you feel fresh and clean insiiiiiiiiide."

"How many?" I asked. "What number will we be?"

"Oh," he said. "About five hundred and sixty-fifth."

At his invitation, we filled our canteens at his spigot outside and walked our bikes the last quarter mile from the pony farm to the Tramping Ground itself, one of Steve's tires having lost pressure and now needing repeated pumpings-up to keep going—no matter, he allowed, as he had a *vulcanizing* kit and he would fix that bad tire once we set up camp and got a fire started. The pony farmer had warned us that likely we would not see the Devil but that "it's a Saturday night and those Campbells that live up in the woods half a mile or so past the Tramping Ground, they'll get to drinking on a Saturday night and when they get to drinking, they like to yell and shoot off guns from the porch. That's the only thing you're likely to hear, so if you do, now you'll know what it is.

"You'll be all right. They don't mean any harm."

We found our way to the vaunted spot of evil spirits, fulminations, and bad plans for mankind. We got a fire going in the center of the big circle (forty feet in diameter), where many a fire had been set before ours, and Steve got to vulcanizing while the rest of us put up our two tents, one to the north and one to the east, on the outer edge of the circle so as to block the Devil should he start his nocturnal strolling. We made sandwiches and told stories and, as "L-L-L-L-L-L-L-L-Linda" was number 1 on the radio Top Ten just then, we tried to sing it, and we discussed how lovely were the Lindas we knew from school. Our remarks were tame and opaque, yet they were laced with deep curiosity and honest yearnings. Steve kept vulcanizing, having nothing but trouble with it, though, and after a while we let the fire die down, poured water on it, and, exhausted, gave up, retired to our tents, and slept soundly.

Till a couple hours later: we woke up startled when one of our number yelled, "The woods are *all lit up!*"

We piled out of our tents and saw the headlights of a big car down by the hard road, pulling up on the shoulder, then backing up, changing its angle, shooting its bright lights up into the woods, the car radio blaring out, and voices too: "You sure this is it?"

"Yeah, this is it."

"Got to be!"

"C'mon."

Some of the voices were men's, some women's—how many were there? Were these the Campbells? There had been no gunfire—yet.

"All right! Bring the beer."

The driver killed the engine, and the car doors opened and slammed shut in quick sequence.

"All right, all right—I *told* you it was *great!*"

"Better be," said one of the women.

Then here they came, up the forty-yard path from the road, flashlights torching through the woods at crazy angles. We stood and watched their enthusiastic approach as one, until they came into the big clearing and their beams struck us and the tents and the energy and drive suddenly went out of their night.

"Well, god-*damn!*"

"Who the hell are *you guys?*"

"We're from Chapel Hill and we're camping here," one of us said.

"The hell!"

"They're just some *boys*," said one of the women.

"From Chapel Hill?" one of the men said.

"That's right."

"Hunh! *We're* the ones from Chapel Hill—U-N-C—and we're *drinking* here!"

"No, we're not," the same woman said again.

"The hell."

"They were here first," said the other woman.

Then the two couples spoke low among themselves, and a cool clarity emerged there near the heart of Lucifer's circle. The college men's amatory plan for these women, driving them an hour to a scary-named spot and drinking beer with them into the night, way out in the Deep Chatham woods, was not going to work, was in fact failing right before our eyes—they had not a one of them come to the Devil's Tramping Ground expecting witnesses, preemptive intruders such as us. Yet here we were, dug in, clearly not leaving.

Best we could tell in the confusion, the flipping-around flashlights, the two women had already turned toward the car and started back down the path.

"Well, god-*damn*," one of the men said, furious, the other adding, "Come all the way down here, and what do we find? A bunch of kids, playing in a sandbox."

"God-*damn.*"

"Devil's Tramping Ground. The hell."

And then, furious and defeated, they were gone.

Milkweed pod

Next day was hot and clear.

Steve could not get his tire patched, so we stopped at the pony farmer's place again and he called his father—the eminent professor E. M. Adams, Virginia tobacco-farm and one-room-schoolhouse raised, at this time chair of UNC's Department of Philosophy—to come pick him and his bicycle up there, and the remaining five of us pedaled on, after a while passing the southbound Dr. Adams (hands gripping hard his Volkswagen steering wheel, teeth clenched, not looking our way at all), just below Siler City. Later in the afternoon, nearing Chapel Hill and on the north upslope above the Haw River at Bynum, another carful of college students (all men) came driving by us, slowing way down as they passed so the passengers could pour a host of cusswords out upon us—then one of them threw a lit firecracker out the window at me, raising a big blood blister where it exploded on my calf.

We all got home, tired and justly proud of our labors—our eighty miles of pedaling and overnighting at the spectral spot—before dark on that warm dogwood spring Sunday. Yet an eerie, cautionary, and unsettling feeling remained with us: twice on our trip we may have met the Devil in the form of a few young men who seemed on the face of it to be, hauntingly, not all that different from us, just a few years older.

Sunflowers

What We Hear

In the field, swallowtails settle on the purplish whorls atop tall stalks of joe-pye weed, a milkweed pod has opened beside our little path down to the lane, where spiderwebs always await us, and the pod's mass of delicate white strands and brown seeds also looks for all the world like it could be a bank for dandelion blowballs. A few okra pods remain on the stalks in the garden, and both light yellow and lavender mums flower like crazy just outside the fence, sunflowers nearby. Small but arrested figs linger and no longer seem to grow and enlarge, while nearby and above, a bumper crop of persimmons ripens. Up the hill, acorns rain down on the deck and hit it and the tin roof with such force that the sounds of a virtual .22 ring out through the woods and over the field. Hickory leaves yellowed by the autumn thus far float down in flights ordered by the lightest of breezes, once again carpeting the lazy-C lane around the hillside field and the forest floor alike.

Fluttering about and landing on the cylinder full of sunflower seeds, the goldfinches and the chickadees, even the yellow-bellied sapsuckers, want a share, and, no less, the cardinals and the mourning doves long for whatever falls onto the squirrel baffle and the ground. The hawk soaring above the field just below the feeder in the woods wants any, or all, of those birds who are in there competing with each other.

The phenomenon of avian variety, of deep-woods birds, is an endless delight. Beyond all those finches, nuthatches, titmice, and gnatcatchers, in turn here come towhees, phoebes, pewees doing their short circular air-dances from high perches, and even the yellow-billed cuckoo, the *rain crow*, celebrated forecaster of weather around Bingham Township—for I have often heard a truism-declaration like this from the dairymen and farmers: "Heard the rain crow just 'fore I come over here—we may get some rain after all, but whether we do or not, you know it'll be raining in Chapel Hill."

So the autumn presses on, arriving with the sweet fruition of October: "the ripe, the golden month has come again," wrote Thomas Wolfe, dramatically celebrating October, his birth month and Ann's and mine too. Libra's time has just about gone, though, and Scorpio is on the move through the cooling air, almost with a vengeance to bring November and winter swiftly on, just as soon as the Full Hunter's Moon is done rising and letting its light fall all over Halloween.

When Ann and I are out walking at sunset and dusk on the long lanes back in the deep woods, we hear a great many things.

We hear cars way out on the two-lane blacktop a mile distant, and also the few of them coming back home our way, crunching over the gravel.

We see and hear deer running, once we spook them ahead of us in the woods and the field.

We hear crows going to roost, the *scree*-ing of hawks on their last hunts of the day, barred owls calling and screeching out to each other, some just across the field, some a half mile away. When Canada geese fly over going to or from the very long Morrow Millpond, honking out in flight, we hear not only their songs but also their big wings beating the air heavily and loudly as they fly above us, not even a hundred feet off the ground.

We hear the reports of pistol shots as target shooters run expensively through their clips rapid-fire, and in the autumn we hear the shotgun *booms* of dove hunters out at cornfield edges only a mile off.

Sometimes lately we hear a pilot off to the southwest flying our way in a motorized parachute, a *paramotor* or *paraplane*, drifting along at twenty-five miles an hour not far above the tree line after taking off in one of the big nearby fields with only a short run, trusting his life to the power of something that looks just like a big house fan.

Fascinating, yet not for us.

We hear the sounds of our own footsteps on dried hickory and oak and sweet gum leaves carpeting the lanes, and we hear more leaves as they fall and strike leaves above, joining the yearly leaf going down to leaf.

And most always we hear the wind in the trees, even when it is scarcely a soughing whisper.

Some late autumn days, and on into the nights if the machinery has headlights, we hear the steady thrumming of the combines cutting away, harvesting the soybeans once they have dried in the fields, and remember when Clayton Rogers was still alive and we could hear him singing old-time hymns full-throated ("*How sweet the sound*") as he drove his tractor, standing up, pulling a harvester. And we hear the cutting going on in the cornfields, too, and later the hum from the Lloydtown dairy a mile away, through the woods to

After the harvest

the west, down across Cane Creek and the woods and fields beyond, where the silage was being augured up into a silo for the herd's feed in winter.

These seasonal sounds are just part of the cycle in a farmland's arena, the sounds of harvest, of husbandry, of plenty.

And even more comforting are the sounds of the animals for whom all this is being done: the gorgeous, bluesy lowing of the dairy cows from across the way, songs of kine for which herders and their families have long been listening out, for so many thousands of years now.

In the night far past dusk, what we hear may be more dire, like the child-like screaming of a rabbit in the talons of an owl. Or something even fiercer: I got home from a show I was doing down in Fayetteville one night about mid-night, and Ann was sitting bolt upright in bed, saucer-eyed, having heard a murderous shrieking from our field below the house only moments before. A countryman I knew once said to me: "When a bobcat howls, it sounds like a woman getting killed."

And more often than we ever would have wished, from the small stream, the unnamed tributary of Cane Creek below the ravine, come the double-helices, the swift-rising howlings of coyotes whose thin, twinned voices rise just as unearthly as those bobcat cries, perhaps more so.

And sometimes we are awakened, feeling before hearing the rapid con-cussive beatings of helicopter rotor blades, as flight squadrons from Pope Air Force Base move their crafts through the Piedmont night, flying over in groups at 1 a.m., 3 a.m., 5 a.m., at times flying so close to the treetops that their blinking lights shine into our bedroom. The owls and geese, the bob-cats and coyotes, are all creatures of these deep Clover Garden woods; but these agile machines, these copters . . .

What is their range, where are they going, and who are they talking to?

How well I recall director-playwright Patrick Tovatt, who hailed from Colorado but had a farm in Kentucky, telling me that coyotes had reached his farm. This was in the early 1980s, and I said, "What do you mean 'reached' and what are you talking about, coyotes in Kentucky?"

"Oh, they're there, all right," he answered, "and they'll be here in North Carolina before you know it."

Much as I doubted that, one morning not too many years afterward, while taking the children to school, there alongside Dairyland Road in a cut cornfield across from the Maple View Dairy and its Holsteins we all saw a slab-sided coyote, standing parallel to the road and paying traffic no mind at all. And John Lane, the keen and inspired poet-naturalist long at Wofford College, nailed the canine's character and presence down in a book about it and in his public pronouncements: "Coyote is here, and he's here to stay!"

After a session of dueling yodeling by two different sets of Clover Garden coyotes one night, I began to wonder if the old pack down past the ravine had produced enough offspring that, not wishing to move too far from home, might now be ensconcing themselves on a different, west-flowing tributary—both streams only an eighth of a mile from our home.

Sometimes coyote yodels come to our ears in harrowing yet beautifully entwined sound, spinning upward in weird blood-chilling harmonies; sometimes they are short, high-trending yips; but they are rarely barks, and coyotes' cryings seem to affect most folks' DNA in ways akin to the hungry, high lonesome howling of wolves—even a bobcat's shriek has more warmth to it.

Being a singer with a sawmill voice, I can hardly begrudge them for singing out, for wanting to and *having* to, and I can admire—on musical levels alone—their pure tones and their truly fabulous ranges.

Yet I can also wish that they were much farther away when they sing at their dens and that they were not feeding regularly on the persimmons fallen off the tree only seventy yards from our back door.

To come halfway up out of sleep at 2 or 3 a.m. and hear the rain starting, falling down through the canopy in earnest upon the tin roof and dripping off the tin onto the pine needles and oak and hickory leaves, I am not only comforted, for we thrive in North Carolina with our almost-fifty inches of rain a year, but thoroughly rewarded, too, simply by being dry and warm inside with Ann. To awaken later at first light and rise just enough to see the big mists the rain is making in the field and hanging in the woods, deer moseying through those mists, one finds oneself in a gray winter's forest, with smoke from our little Upland woodstove falling down the slope, mixing with the rain, drifting into the field, and melding with the mists there.

The Danes have a saying for such spectral moments: "The Bog Witch is brewing."

What We See

Midmorning in December, and light mists from last night's rain still hung like faint gray shrouds in the winter woods, and the tawny sedges in the field stood brightly against the gloomy day.

The goldfinches seem to have taken flight and migrated several weeks back, though the nuthatches and titmice, chickadees and juncos were hitting the sunflower-seed feeder with delight and abandon, except when one particularly hungry yellow-bellied woodpecker, the size of four or five of the smaller birds together, boomed into the yard and the small ones would all scatter. A few days before, a sharp-shinned hawk did his own booming in, picking off a songbird in the process and sitting in a dogwood not twenty feet from our deck to dine upon it.

In a few weeks, the goldfinches will have returned. Ann looked out at the bird feeder early one fifteen-degree morning the day after Christmas and saw no birds moving yet and only a couple of deer looking for uneaten sunflower seeds among the hulls on the ground. Pretty soon, the sunny day warmed, if only slightly, and goldfinches (back from where?) started showing up, coming at the feeder as wrathily as they might have in midsummer and energetically knocking each other off the several perches on the small feeder's column.

Years ago, a young sharp-shinned hawk had glided easily into the yard from the field and gone after a totally exposed young squirrel and nearly snagged it, but the squirrel at the last moment ran under our picnic table, while the frustrated hawk landed atop it. For the next twenty minutes, the hawk paced back and forth along the eight-foot length of the table, while the upward-looking squirrel moved beneath it in directions opposite to the hawk's. Those moments offered a rare and special view into the practical psychology of predator and prey, and ere long the hawk, thoroughly disappointed, which is anthropomorphic for *outwaited*, flew back out into the field to look for other morsels not shielded by tables.

Ann and I were sitting on the screened porch one morning when two immature pileated woodpeckers flew close by, landing on an oak and a hickory growing only a few feet apart and only a scant twenty feet from where we sat. For most of half an hour they rose up the tree trunks on slow spirals, more helices in the wild, always keeping each other in sight and giving us the best lengthy look we had ever had at the oft-heard, rarely seen royalty of the deep woods. For us, only an unusual time with a patient, worm-digging pileated woodpecker on a large lot on Bridge Street in Columbia, North Carolina, two blocks from the Scuppernong River, even came close.

What was a young possum doing at the base of our sunflower-seed bird feeder there in the yard, lying dead, without any visible or obvious wounds? Ultimately, the only thing that made sense was that he climbed the pole, grasped for the unclimbable metal baffle at the feeder's base, fell over backward, and broke his neck. We left him there till we knew for sure he was not playing possum, then carried him with a shovel down into the field, where the buzzards would find him in their own good time, and be grateful, or, at least, fed.

On a recent cold Christmastide night, when daughter Cary was home from the North, she said she had heard someone walking through the woods. "I looked out the upstairs window with the flashlight to see . . . a possum," Cary reported. "And then the possum hissed and from the darkness I heard 'hiss

hiss' right back, and there was an enormous raccoon. And then they both went running off in different directions!"

An unusual trilling drew Ann to the screen porch late one recent summer night after a massive cloud-buster, and just as she dropped a beam of light on a mature raccoon and its two babies, who turned out to be the trillers, an unseen bobcat nearby frightened her deeply with its single savage snarl.

"Children of the night," the enraptured Romanian actor Bela Lugosi, inimitable as Count Dracula, declared appreciatively of singing wolves: "What music they make."

On a mid-August Tuesday last year, when a mighty and forceful west wind, a squall line in essence, passed through both Triad and Triangle, Ann stood at our home office window watching the wind pressing down the very large azaleas (which normally reached eight feet tall but before the wind were now down to three feet) and while watching that effect saw from the corner of her eye a fifty-foot pine come down at an oblique angle to our house barely forty feet away: astonishment and relief. The next evening from that same window she observed four rabbits scooting under those same azaleas, which would not have given them much comfort or cover only twenty-four hours earlier . . . as Dinah Washington sang, "What a difference a day makes!"

I was once at the very window when motion on the porch outside caught my eye. A fledgling wren had hopped out of its nest in the Garden Way cart up onto the cart's upper edge, where it sat as I watched it for about half a minute, after which it flew in that mighty flapping and slow-forward-motion way that fledglings do. Into the large azalea bush a dozen feet from my window, it flapped.

And then came a second wren, up from the nest and perching in the same place, though not waiting quite as long to fly in that humorously clumsy fashion on into the azalea. Then a third, then a fourth, each of these two hardly waiting at all before they flew and joined the others.

I went out onto the front porch, where I could watch the four little wrens enlarge their world, which they soon did by flying back and forth among the original azalea and a thicket of others some thirty feet away. Had I not lingered, bemused, I would have missed one of the most unusual sights ever granted me back in these woods.

Over the next ten minutes, as the young wrens were cavorting and loving it, a remarkable, unmatched flock of older birds—an audience—formed up in the trees above: cardinals, bluebirds, robins, a mockingbird or two. These elders were drawn there by the same thing that had drawn me out: to watch fledglings work out with their newfound agility and freedom, to watch them in their astonishment, unknowing as to how they might have sprouted wings and flown but now feeling, simply feeling the glory of it, while the elders regarded them in endorsement and, too, with a sense of protection about them, in what had to have been a pure-form avian celebration of youth in the state of nature.

Only once have I ever seen this.

Stars

Because Clover Garden lies midway east-west between Chapel Hill–Carrboro and Graham, and likewise north-south between Hillsborough and Pittsboro, no significant sky glow from any of these towns alters or impedes our excellent views of the night sky. Not to be overselling our evening and nocturnal heavens—to see anything truly worthy of the full dark sky sobriquet, one must travel out to the Carolina coast, to the pocosins or Ocracoke or Core Banks, though Jordan Lake and the Uwharrie Mountains also offer us highly appealing central North Carolina night skies. And in the mountains, the bare, dark heavens above Mayland's Earth to Sky Park and Observatory close to Burnsville await us. Yet Ann and I love to stop at the top of our field after walking the lane and look out for Venus and to sit on the porch deck and see which planets are popping out after the sun has disappeared beyond the oaks and hickories and pines. And many is the time we have set an alarm for two or three in the morning, then bundled the children and ourselves up and walked down into the frigid field to see how many shooting stars light up the cold, dark sky during the Geminids meteor showers of December, or the easier warmer nights of the Perseids of August, or the Lyrids of April that light up the spring around the time of Shakespeare's birthday.

Many times the falling star makes only a small thin line of light for scarcely a second, yet at other moments the meteorite seems to be moving slowly enough and big enough that its burning disintegration appears against the night sky as vividly as a matchstick flaring along the striker, always as a surprise, since not a one of us can predict where and when the next star will fall.

What a gift to have been given, way back in childhood down near the Pasquotank River in eastern Carolina, when my father first set me to looking toward the moon through his father's telescope. I saw more falling stars, of course, with my naked eyes than I ever did with that beloved three-piece brass spyglass. When my grandmother Simpson sent me a small two-piece telescope with a tiny tripod for Christmas when I was about eleven, I was overjoyed, and still recall setting it up, turning it toward a penumbral lunar eclipse late one December night in 1963.

Perhaps we still do all this walking out and watching our skies, however dark they may be, waiting in faith for the meteorites to shower down because some-one older whom we loved unconditionally once sang to us a lovely, if loony, imperative—*Catch a falling star and put it in your pocket, never let it fade away*—and thereby bidding us from an early age to keep a watch, always to keep a watch, and to see if we really could catch falling stars, little orbs that might somehow really fit into our pockets and not burn them but just sit there glowing, waiting till the someday when we might need them, never ever fading away.

Riderless Horse

A few evenings after Christmas one year, a few of us (Ann; her sister Carolyn; her cousin Sally; our son, Hunter; our daughter Cary; and I) stepped out of the cottage and walked lazily down to the field, heading for the lane and a long walk. We got started a bit late for it, though, as the cold, cloudy winter's day was darkening quickly.

We had not gotten halfway down the field when we were stopped in our tracks by what we saw entering the field's lower entrance: A riderless horse.

On up toward us the dark horse came, docile, it seemed, slow-gaited, easy-mannered, and when he stopped and stood still, I took his reins and we six spoke anxiously. The woods were deep, the hour late—it would be dusk in a few minutes, fully dark in less than an hour.

The rider could be anywhere in these hundreds of acres of woods, injured: a sprained ankle or hurt leg, a concussion, almost any injury could keep a wounded rider from finding his or her way out of the big woods to safety.

And the cold would be dropping into the twenties on this night.

Quickly, I called the sheriff's headquarters and reported that we had someone's lost horse. And that we feared for the lost rider.

Then we waited as the dusky dark came on.

As good fortune had it, our wait would not be long.

A black pickup truck rolled up the lane and stopped at the lower opening, and a blonde woman in boots and jeans and a cowboy hat stepped out of the passenger door and shouted up at us: "That's my horse!"

She operated Hideaway Stable not a mile down the slopes toward Cane Creek from us, and she walked up and said she had the horse saddled and ready for a late afternoon rider intent on a short canter—but the horse had

Beech bough

other ideas, and before the rider could mount him, he ran off up the road in our direction, turning in on our main lane. When she had called the sheriff, the word from us was already there, and she acted at once. Our visions of a rider lying injured in the woods on a frigid night would not come to pass, after all, though how often that very thing must have happened in the immemorial wilds of our pine barrens, our Piedmont, our pinnacled world.

The black pickup turned around and drove off, and the stable woman patted the horse's big neck and climbed up on him, turning to us as she rode away, all of us knowing she and the great animal would be scarcely a silhouette in the last light by the time she got back down Morrow Mill Road to her stables, unsaddled him, and hung up the tack and cooled him down.

"Thank you," she said, smiling. "From me *and* my horse."

Beech

These are the raw, bitter-cold days of February, days when the high might be anywhere from thirty-three to forty-six degrees, dispersed across the month between just a few spare outlying days of promising balm and

warmth. Most always these are days that can feel like they are hovering right
at the ice point—especially when enforced by extremely fine, penetrating mists to create a true brutal cold.

We do know that in recent years the redbud has shown its first scant blossoms on the eighteenth of February, a full day earlier than the prior year's appearance on the nineteenth, most of a month ahead of blooming time in the old days. Daffodils too can hold back no more, nor dwarf iris, and forsythia comes yellowing out, maples reddening up, wild onions showing on roadsides and ditch banks.

And yet, when a week of February rain comes, as it has here during the moment of the Full Snow Moon, the deep woods are dark gray and foreboding, and one may feel portioned off, isolated, as Major de Spain's bear-hunting crowd was in Faulkner's fictional big-woods Yokna Bottoms most of a century and a half ago—cold, colder, unprovisioned, with nothing warming left to drink.

Only the beech trees and their marcescent leaves, looking like sand or wheat, bring light to such dark, wet woods, standing out vividly among the dark-gray oak and hickory trunks and the cyanine green of the cedars. A few of our beech trees are large and well spread out, but many more are saplings, six to twelve feet high, present and proud and serving as fine, multifaceted reflectors.

Naturalist Tom Earnhardt calls them "one of Tar Heelia's most noble trees. . . . They are literally found from the mountains to the coast. I know of one 'dwarf beech forest' on top of Elk Knob (almost 6,000 feet)—beech trees that are stunted by the wind and cold. They also grow along the Chowan, the Roanoke, and in Nags Head Woods.

"And I agree with you," Tom adds, "that the golden leaves of the beech tree in winter are a source of light in the forests. Beech is also a major source of fat and protein, in the form of beech nuts, for many species of wildlife." Though beech scale insects affect these trees from Maine to Wisconsin to our Carolina mountains, we note that this serious affliction is not in our Piedmont beech forests.

The northern side of the beech forest nearest us, from our Clover Garden field a quarter mile on out to Cane Creek, was once as open as open can be beneath a mature beech canopy, till Hurricane Fran's topside, northwest winds came in, bearing down counterclockwise on central Carolina, and this big beech wood fell before them.

Oh, she had a field day here, Fran did, back in 1996. Two weeks of rain, before she curved along north of the Bahamas, gave her license to set her 120-mile-an-hour sights on Wilmington and the Cape Fear valley—Fran's winds were so mighty, and this big beech wood just to our north fell before them, and that was the ruin of the broad open wood.

And soon those coyotes were roaming the bramble that grew up in Fran's aftermath, denning on the slender stream that came flowing forth from the springs below our flatwoods and running on out to Cane Creek, singing their hair-raising, woeful songs.

(*opposite*)
Cane Creek
in winter

A timber outfit soon appeared, there to clean up the hardest-hit portions of the beech forest, on the early twentieth-century Gold Mine Tract just to our north. When I saw from my office window a feller buncher at work in the ravine, our border, I ran into that ancient draw and pulled out as many pieces as I could of the collapsed split-rail fence there, the old bright zig-zag wooden stitching against the dead leaves of the forest floor, which had penned in Morrow Farm hogs a century ago. We later lined those lengths around a half a dozen azaleas, a big oak, and a big hickory, where the young pileated woodpeckers played that morning.

On our side of the ravine, our southwestern slope, we lost but a single large beech to Fran, and in coming years we saw that the lamp-like qualities of the beech in no way depended upon their size, the smaller trees shining just as brightly and vividly as the larger ones. Poet Evan Gurney and I spoke of this on the Carolina campus one day, as we reported to each other our walks at sundown and dusk—we thought the late autumnal beech had been particularly luminous that fall, and perhaps they were, or perhaps we had just seen them in this different way and valued them anew.

We have heard that the Danes, at the first blush of spring in that far-north land, make communal pilgrimages into the open understory of the beech woods there. Hans Christian Andersen celebrated Denmark's "agreeable hills [that] rise covered with vast beech-woods," and since one tree of every three in Denmark is a European beech, emblematic of longevity and strength, this really is their national tree.

Recently, we were fortunate enough to wander into the almost 14,000 acres of Gribskov, or Gribs Forest, in Zealand—one of the last "vast beech-woods" remaining in Denmark and a remnant of the so-called *tangle* that once covered the country. During World War II, the British Royal Air Force often parachuted arms by night down to the waiting Danish resistance fighters here, who were invisible in the dark and, as the mature beech trees in Gribskov have diameters of two to three feet or more at breast height, on the rolling ground below beneath a *very* thorough, often interlacing, canopy.

❀ ❀ ❀

One New Year's Day, Ann, Bill Garlick, and I walked in late afternoon out toward Cane Creek, out to a fifty- to sixty-foot sharp rise above our flattening ravine, below which that hillside let water seep out and form several springs, which quickly coalesced, starting a narrow tributary out to Cane Creek a quarter mile to the north. We followed an old logging road in that direction, soon high above the falling stream, through a forest of young and mature beech grown low enough in this hilly land that they seemed to have been left untouched by Hurricane Fran way back.

By the time we had walked down onto the Cane Creek floodplain, some sixty to eighty yards wide from stream to rise, we three had really gotten into a serious strolling mood, so we started upstream on a deer path hard by the creek, past an enormous rock headland, one stretch of the path so narrow and slick and angled creek-ward that a single unbalanced slip on the trail's damp leaves would put one directly into Cane Creek's slow-moving winter waters eight feet below.

Once past this challenge, I turned back to look, with far better fortune than Lot's wife, at the western sun—still up about ten degrees, shining and casting long, pure, golden light upon all the beech trees behind us, the big elders and the blithe saplings, our wintry lanterns all lit up.

And now we are back again in February, and I see the beech trees from where I sit as the only glow in the foggy, rain-misted woods. A truly remarkable sight: because they hold their crisp blond dead leaves after fall's fade, and hold them over all the months between November and February, the beech rattle in the cold breezes and, ironically and alone in all the forest, shine on—and shine out—all winter long and, so glowing, offer us light and hope and timely faith that spring will, as always, come again soon.

Turkeys

Late one spring morning about thirty-odd years ago, as I sat working in the bright, window-cornered portion of our living room, something moving outside caught my eye, and I looked up and saw a guinea hen or two pecking in the tall grass at the center of our field just down the slope.

Whose guineas are they? I wondered.

More than a couple, though—five or ten, no, twenty, I thought, as I saw more of them in the grass, quickly putting on my glasses and counting.

Thirty, at least.

Yet now, as my heart pounded, I could see they were not guineas at all.

Wild turkeys—more than I had ever seen at one time in my life, and they were slowly pecking at insects as they moved northwest across the field. I stood stock-still—for they are warier than deer and have the keenest hearing. If I moved a bit in the house and they heard, they would all be gone in a heartbeat.

Turkey after turkey raised its head high, looked about, then bowed down into the fescue, feeding, or trying to feed, all of them taking their time as they moved, twenty minutes in all from when I had first noticed them till the last one disappeared.

Immediately, excitedly, I called Fred Summers down at the old Morrow Mill on Cane Creek and told him what I had just witnessed, and he confirmed with his own excitement and wonder: "Yep, I've been seeing 'em too this past week, pecking around my garden area here at the mill."

I thought about the mother and her six poults that Frank Queen and I saw one time up on the ridge in Austin's Quarter when we were gathering firewood, the single male that Jake and I, out squirrel hunting, flushed out of a short oak on the hilltop a hundred yards or so up behind our house.

Many years later, east of Kinston and Wyse Fork, driving out of the short span of wet woods called Tracey Swamp, Ann and I saw the flooded swamp waters standing in the field a good ways south of the highway, and there at the back of that harvested cornfield we also saw about sixty wild turkeys all flocked up, pecking at the soaked land in obvious feasting on whatever else the flood had forced up to higher ground.

Sixty!

Quite the sight, especially in a state whose entire wild turkey population was down to 2,000 birds only fifty years ago. Today there are well over a quarter million of them in North Carolina, a tremendous avian conservation victory, a great collaboration between North Carolina's Wildlife Resources folks and the turkey hunters themselves.

Not too long after that, out walking ever more often in the early evenings, Ann and I began to see small sequential patches of rustled-up leaves for twenty or thirty yards here and there right alongside our gravel lane, as if something had been on the run along the lane and veered to its edge now and again and roughed it up.

Deer?

Coyotes after deer?

We had plenty of them denning down on the stream below the ravine, but why would large running quadrupeds come just off the gravel lane? And if they did, why were the leaves bunched and not scattered, and why were there no tracks?

We called on the renowned farrier George Terll of Chatham County, probably the best all-around outdoorsman in our ken, who would know from instinct and experience, for sure. As soon as I sent George a photo of a line of diggings, he said that yes, those were tom turkeys out looking for mates, spring of the year, hungry all the time, trying to find something easy to pull up out of the leaf litter.

"And you'll never see them," he said, adding, "Even though they're there!"

Floating the Deep

The moving waters at their priestlike task . . .
—John Keats, "Bright Star"

So it was that on March days some years apart, the great coastal historian David Cecelski and I floated three Deep River runs between Carbonton and down to below Cumnock, from lower run to upper in order, starting one gray morning in March 2008. Our put-in would be at the well-known camel-back bridge at Cumnock, now part of a beloved local park, with a take-out down a dirt lane on the upstream side of the old 15–501 bridge over the Deep, miles north of Sanford.

First leaving David's jeep up under that bridge, we then drove my station wagon a ways above the north side of the river toward Cumnock, and, as we were in the more-or-less heart of the old Chatham County coal country (a belt in Chatham and Lee including such communities as Goldston and Egypt, covering much the same territory in recent times envisioned, shortsightedly, for potential future hydraulic fracturing operations) from earlier times, we took a side trip to the site of the Coal Glen mine that blew up in 1925, an awful disaster that killed fifty-three men.

Now on the coal mine's site stood a modest wood-treatment plant, and one would scarcely think that here in this place occurred the tragic end of so many men, the ruin of so many families. Journalist, author, and future Lost Colony publicist Ben Dixon MacNeill covered that tragedy, and his prose and photographs told the hideous story of the day, for he watched thousands of people troop by to see the scene and pay tribute, even a bizarre truckload of college students from Chapel Hill who showed up in a picnicking mood "as for a holiday, elbowing their way in among the drawn-faced mothers who watched for the coming up of their sons. They were quieted by the spectacle."

Women chopping cotton at a nearby farm had heard the explosions and saw the billowing black coal-smoke filling the air. Only one miner escaped death, because his cow had gotten loose that morning, and he had gone after it and not down into the dark-as-a-dungeon shafts where he made his living. A seven-year-old farmer's daughter, Margaret Wicker, had borne witness to the whole sad affair and had once told David Cecelski, when he was interviewing folks for his column "Listening for a Change," that there were not enough coffins to bury all the dead and they just had to wait. She said it took a week to get all the bodies out.

MacNeill back in 1925 called it all "a monstrous sorrow."

The Deep sat down in a trough with banks twenty feet high, hence the river's name, and we floated easily along in the white canoe for a while, keeping our eyes keen for the Civil War era Furnace of Endor, which once produced iron for the Confederate arsenal down in Fayetteville. At a spot with low banks, we stopped and had a sandwich up on a hillside fifty yards from the river's edge, then braved a narrow channel and rapids and went on.

As neither of us had ever seen the Furnace of Endor, every mound and pile of debris we passed had us guessing—Could *that* be it? How could we have missed it? Till finally we spied the thirty-five-foot-tall rock tower set back in the woods from the river's south bank, and we knew there would have been *no* missing this creation: smart brown masonry, rough-cut grayish-red stones, with a semicircled smelting-oven opening at its base, its falling-in top an angled ruin. It held the sort of wonder that had an Ozymandian *look on my works, ye mighty* quality to it: once important, now nothing but a curiosity, this huge ruin.

David and I are both innately cheerful men, though given to somber reflection when face-to-face with object lessons of the past. As we had paused earlier at the now-effaced Coal Glen site, we gave this old stove-in monument a good hard look before rejoining the river.

Soon, in brilliant afternoon sunlight, a mountain rose ahead of us resplendently, and beneath its beauty we paddled to the next bridge in good spirits indeed. There our last maritime action of the day was hearty, if comical. We had a truly hard climb up the slick muddy bank, holding onto grass, quite literally grasping at straws to gain just enough lift to make it up twelve feet to the top. Then, after getting the canoe's tie-down straps from David's jeep and hitching them to the forward canoe-seat thwarts, the two of us climbed the bank a second time, now from above pulling the white canoe upward, we two men moving together exactly as mules, to its near-vertical take-out, a singular moment among the many wonderful times we have shared afloat and afield.

Our second March day on the Deep, David and I met in Gulf, intending to run downriver to the camel-back bridge in Cumnock. At the general store on US 421, which sported everything from tractor parts to ice cream to children's toys, a man there led us outside and said, "You all know of Charlie Daniels?"

"Sure," we said. "'The Devil Went Down to Georgia'!"

"That's right, that boy can flat play the fiddle! Well, he grew up right there in that house over yonder."

So with Big Charlie's "Fire on the mountain, run, boys, run, / Devil's in the house of the rising sun" in our heads, we drove across the road to the Triangle Land Conservancy's McIver Landing, where a steep forested (and staircased) bluff led down to the brown river: Gulf, a turning basin and head of navigation in a past era of river commerce.

The Deep first and immediately ran us and the white canoe over a Class I rapids and then veered way off to the west. Quickly we were far away from the big highway and its noise, and before long, we gazed upon huge, dark, dramatic rock outcrops that banked the stream's west side and went gliding beside and beneath them.

After paddling beneath a high railroad trestle bridging the Deep, we tied up to the bank and ate sandwiches without ever leaving the canoe. And then we ran right alongside the railroad grade for a good spell and at last took out just past the camel-back bridge at Cumnock, familiar ground.

The old Carbonton dam has long since been done away with—knocked apart and carted off soon after power generation ended here in 2004, part of a dam-decommissioning movement reminiscent of the celebrated 2017 removal of Milburnie Dam on the Neuse River. We slid the two canoes (David and his daughter Vera's green one, Ann's and my white one) and David's son Guy's kayak past the willows and over the riverine mudflat beside the old, tall brick and concrete powerhouse—all that was left of the dam's former operation—and took off downriver on the Deep toward Gulf, and a cold March morning it was.

Again we ate lunch in the boats. This run was one of long reaches, till near the end when we moved swiftly into some fast-running bends, the river waters rippling and at times almost roaring over reedbeds along the insides of curves.

Deep River at confluence with Rocky River, looking downstream, White Pines Preserve, Chatham County

The take-out at Gulf appeared much steeper this day than it had the earlier time we put in there at the foot of the flight of stairs. Yet came a miracle of the bright and young: Guy and Vera literally took the white canoe out of Ann's and my hands and lofted it up those stairs, along a walkway and up more stairs, to the Triangle Land Conservancy's parking area there at McIver Landing. And we gave great thanks to them and to TLC, which had kindly put these amenities in place for just such river-running souls as we five.

Our neighbor Dale Williams, an active older man with a ready smile and always a story, whom we know from Beaufort, grew up on a Rocky River horse farm and loved it: the stables, the tack, the hay and other feed, and, naturally, the animals themselves. The farm was not too far up the Rocky

Wild iris

from its confluence with the Deep, and he used to saddle up and ride down the river to that meeting of the waters. There the big dark rocks protruded in all but flood times, and light-green freshwater marshes grew around and over them as the Deep River headed on to its own joining with Haw River at Mermaid Point, the starting spot of the great, wild Cape Fear.

The floodplain at the Deep and Rocky's point of confluence is significant, though not large, perhaps 150 yards wide and 60 or 80 yards deep. And the river-end of a very steep ridge-head looms up and over that flat.

When Ann and I told Dale about our sterling afternoon walking out that long ridge to find "the moving waters at their priestlike task," as Keats wrote—all part of the Triangle Land Conservancy's White Pines Preserve—Dale laughed and said that as a boy he used to love to ride a horse down to the point, then up the ridge end facing them and on into the high white pines above.

"How'd the horse like that?" I asked him.

"Oh, man," he laughed even more. "He'd lean into it, and he'd dig and dig and *dig* to get up the side of that hill! That was some *fun*." Dale's old pal Mike Blackwell told me he was once in that confluence floodplain with a group of twenty on horseback and that few wanted to try the climb.

"I had a big horse named Whisky and rode him to the hill and said, 'Git it, Whisky!' And up he went, got to the top and just *shook himself!*"

Perhaps there are boys and girls and horses still doing that—there must be in the hills and plains of horsey Carolina—if not exactly at Dale's old riverside adventure spot, though I can see him and his horse at work on that trail long ago, climbing the contours, the fierce concentration of tendon and blood and hoof lifting them to a higher realm, where the clean, astringent smell of the pines met and welcomed them always and where the forest holding the high ground gave boy and horse a slowly ascending, easy going along the ridge, all the way back to the family farm.

Another day Dale Williams told us a Deep and Rocky River tale of a rather different nature, how on Tuesday, May 26, 1925, Dale's grandfather had walked into the office of the Coal Glen Mining Company after his shift was done and told the boss man that he would not be back, that today would be his last day underground, and that he was going to make a big garden this summer and farm.

And then he went on home to his wife.

The very next day, the dust below ground ignited and blew up the Coal Glen mine. Men, women, and children waited at the head of the mine shaft, waiting and praying all the week that it took to retrieve all the miners who had died.

And Dale's grandmother, a young nurse whose husband but for fortune might have been among them, all week long helped tend to the dead, as they were brought up so slowly from that deep, dark world.

For a few more miles, over marshes, rocks, and shallows and a dam, the Deep goes it alone, then meets up with the Haw and forms the mighty Cape Fear River. The very old-time English nomenclaturists tried Cape Fair (sometimes Fayre) and thus Cape Fair River, but that did not stick, any more than the naming by Spanish explorers, well before the English, who called it Rio Jordan.

But *Fear* stuck. Cape Fear for the last J-hook point of sand down at Bald Head Island by the sea. Cape Fear River for the main drain, its basin entirely within North Carolina's borders, bringing its brown waters to the Cape itself.

At the confluence of Deep and Haw once stood a tavern, presiding over the head of the Cape Fear River and controlling its tales and the credulous rivermen who believed them and retold them not because they were true but because the men as always and forever *wanted* them to be true. The tavern's spot between the meeting place of Deep and Haw, they all called Mermaid Point: the place to where all the mermaids swam up from the Carolina coast, to bathe and rest and sleep in their state of nature in the moonlight, just a little closer to the river waters than the tavern itself. And the tavern keepers over time knew they needed those mermaids nearby just as much as the lonely and desirous boatmen who happened by and came through the rude door and threw down real coin for whatever corn beer or stump-hole whiskey the old tavern had to offer.

Boatmen dance, boatmen sing, boatmen do most anything . . .

So the tavern keepers made the men (they were only and always men) a promise honored entirely in the breach: *You may not see them when you're snubbing up to shore and tying off lines and making your way in here, but you stay awhile, warm yourself by the fire here, have a drink, have another, what's your hurry, and let dusky dark and then true dark come on, and after a while the moon'll rise, she's full or most full of an evening now, and then have one for the river, and when you leave and make your way through the brush and the mud back down to your boat, then you will see the mermaids, fair enough, in the bright cold moonlight, lying in the marsh grass at the point and the sedge in the shallows, and when you hear them, you will know . . .*

That those are mermaids calling and singing out, and they are calling just for you, believe it, on this night of nights they are calling for you, yes, just for you, and for you alone.

A Carol for Cane Creek

"Sure are running through your wood there."

"Yes, sir," I said.

The old dairyman Mr. Bob Kirk and I stood in an open pole barn on a hilltop in Orange Grove, several miles north of Clover Garden. It was late in the day and I was captain of the fire barrels for the big Cane Creek community pig-cooks we had in Bingham Township back in the late 1970s and early 1980s, in the spring and fall of the year and again at Christmas.

"When's the meat go on?"

"Eight."

Orange Grove

"Who's bringing it—Thomas?"

"Thomas and Charles," I said.

"You gon' fire all these cookers?"

"Yes, sir."

"All six of 'em?"

"Yes, sir."

"What time'd you light those barrels?"

"Five." The rusty oil drums, stuffed with hickory both green and seasoned, got lit at five on the absolute dot or there would be no pig-cooking. Fred Summers's orders.

"Well, ain't but six-fifteen now," he said, as I threw another couple of split hickory pieces into each barrel. "I don't believe that wood's gon' last you all night."

The dairyman, one of the older farmers in the community, always stopped by to see what was going on and to admonish me about the fuel supply. We

Cane Creek Farms stand just north of Orange Grove

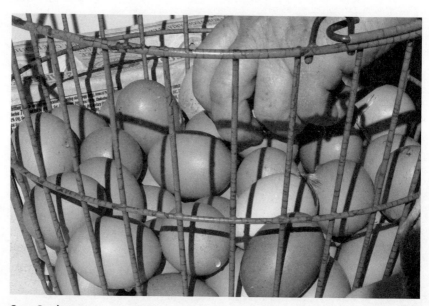

Cane Creek eggs

had had this talk well over a dozen times during my tenure as fire barrel captain. After I was fully warned, he generally offered me a Miller from his cooler, and we would stand and sip in silence.

It would be good and dusky now, the two barrels really going. When neither of us spoke, the windy rush of the fire and the steaming green wood were the only sounds. Now and then we could hear the Holsteins lowing from the dairy down the broad slope. The clean air would get brisk, and we would move a few steps closer to the barrels. Then with little ado the dairyman would head for his pickup, calling back one last time: "Best go easy on that wood, now. You don't want to *waste* any."

Another who helped me keep the watch was the blacksmith who stopped on his way from his forge in Hillsborough to his home at Dodson's Crossroads. Paul Gove looked like Kit Carson, with a wide mustache and a floppy leather hat and fringed leather coat, his face black from the forge and his eyes rimmed with soot. Half the people around the Clover Garden and Orange Grove area with woodstoves or fireplaces seemed to have iron fireplace tools that he had wrought.

We sat in lawn chairs and, through a small rectangular window cut out of each barrel's bottom, we watched the coals collect. Paul most always held an unlit Tampa Jewel, and I just kept on burning wood. Every now and again I clanged a shovel against the sides of the barrels to make the wood settle, and hot swarms of sparks flew out the top.

Paul would reflect on how he and collaborator Jim Walker made fireworks, telling me in great and familiar detail about which chemicals mixed together made what colors and how and why their colors were such subtle, beautiful pastels.

"Serious pyrotechnics," he drawled. He and Jim were responsible for the increasingly popular Fourth of July fireworks down in northern Chatham County, and he told me they were going to have to move it from Chicken Bridge to Frosty's Trading Post, a couple miles south, the next year (and I told him we would be there, and we were).

"It's got too big," he said. "You just can't keep the riffraff out."

Right about eight o'clock Thomas and Charles, both longtime dairymen, always showed up with the pork, in the early years whole hogs, but more often than not boxes of shoulders.

The Centurion

Once there was a pig dressed out but with an ear still on it, and Charles insisted that had to go.

"Maybe this knife'll do the trick," he said, going after the hog's hide with a tiny penknife. When that failed, he went to the only other blade around, an axe. He got the pig onto his truck's tailgate, but when he raised the axe he hit the camper-shell window on the upswing. He choked up on the axe handle and managed to club, if not cut, the offending ear off the carcass. The axe blade even on a short-arc swing made a ring on that tailgate you could have heard for a mile.

"Fire the cookers!" came Fred's cry.

Into the openings of the barrels we skidded the shovels, then carried glowing mounds of coals to each metal fuel-tank cooker in turn. Through little hinged doors on their sides or ends we scattered the coals about the bottoms. As soon as the cookers started smoking at the seams, we opened them up and laid the pork out all over the grills within.

For the next ten hours, this was the drill: one or two men kept a constant check on the cookers to make sure they stayed hot enough. The way they told the temperature was by laying hands (briefly) on top of the cookers. This was the only thermometer we ever used.

Each of these hulking homemade ovens—old oil tanks laid over on their sides on two-wheeled trailers—bore the name of its owner. If one of the checkers cried out, "Charles is cold! More fire to Charles!" then one of us shovelers spread more coals around inside Charles's cooker.

"Now Thomas! Thomas 'bout gone out."

Lanky Ed Johnson, a fine and much-loved Bingham Township community leader, son of the renowned UNC sociologists Guy and Guion Johnson and a psychology professor of note himself at Carolina, always looked in on us. More people showed up, some men and women to work on into the night, some just to visit. Shovels clanged against the barrels and sparks swirled up into the night as the shovelers kept shaking coals down to the barrel bottoms. The coal carriers hurried to the biggest and best of the cookers, inspired by the urgency of the infield chatter: "For God's sake, somebody get some fire to Fred!"

Fred Summers the man, as distinguished from the big Fred cooker (built by Lewis Allen and later named the Centurion) with the green angle-iron frame, wanted no more fire than he already had. Most of the world knew Fred as an ob-gyn in Durham and his wife, Marie, as the abundantly spirited and inspired operator of a successful pottery studio and kiln, but to us Fred was for many years the point man of the whole pig-cook. A short, rounded man, he always wore his baggy scrubs and a small straw hat with a ridged peak fore to aft.

More a lord of mischief than misrule, it was Fred Summers who also led us in the tossing of wine bottles off Eric and Miggie Schopler's deck after dinners there, toward the Joanna Hole in Cane Creek fifty or sixty feet down below. He would have carefully placed a stamped return postcard addressed to him (and with his phone number) into the bottle, along with a dollar to encourage the finder to answer the questions on the card and mail it (where did you find the bottle, what were you doing when you found it, were you clothed or naked at the time?), and sealed the aperture and bottleneck with duct tape.

Over the years, Fred's inspired hydrological experiment sustained its popularity, and no one kept count of the scores of bottles pitched off into the creek, all on faith, as the response rate was zero.

Till one night at Fred and Marie's, at a dinner party of Clover Garden neighbors in the old Morrow Mill, the phone rang and Fred took it (he was on call), and the caller said he had found our bottle and that he was filing his report:

He had lifted it from the surf at Carolina Beach, he said, and Fred repeated this at once to all at the dinner table. This was incredible, and we were riotous—the bottle had made it down Cane Creek to the Haw, had survived the Haw's rocky rapids, gotten past the Jordan Lake dam at Moncure, gone on by Mermaid Point, and then: over, through, and past *three* locks the Corps maintains on the Cape Fear, past Wilmington, past Southport and Bald Head Island and the great Cape Fear itself, into the Atlantic after a 200-mile float, and now over Frying Pan Shoals and up our coastline thirteen more miles to where the caller had found our bottle!

The man told Fred he had been surf-casting when he spied the bottle, but when Fred asked him the final question—were you clothed or naked?—the fisherman said he had told Fred everything he needed to know, said thanks for the dollar, and then quickly rang off.

Once, after Fred had lost a fair bit of weight, Thomas sized him up from behind and asked: "Fred, how long you say it's been since that family moved out of the seat of your pants?"

The dairymen were always interested in breeding stock, especially if they could discuss it in such a way that held the interest of the women at these big open-air events. They would carry on about sperm ampoules and hormone implants and breeding gloves. They would invariably work their conversation around to where they needed an opinion from the one among us who knew a great deal about humans and reproduction.

"Now, Fred, you're a baby doctor," someone would say. "How come it is that . . . ?"

"I am *not* a baby doctor," he would remind the barbeque assembly. "I'm a *woman* doctor!"

People in the long-night business of a pig-cook, enveloped as we were by clouds of pork smoke, tended to grow hungry. Along about 1 or 2 a.m., Fred always had side dishes baking away beside the pork shoulders in the ovens: eight or ten chickens, all slathered down with hot vinegar sauce, and chicken livers and gizzards. For a while there was talk of barbequeing a goat, but there was no mandate for it decades ago (though the feeling about goats would change in time, with more Hispanic folks moving into the area), and the idea fell away.

There once was a hog tongue, though, once again Fred's doing. He suffered much noisy outrage and abuse as he extracted it from the pig it came with, then parboiled and skinned it before barbequeing it to what he swore would be perfection. Even in rustic surrounds, Fred had a flair—he had a stone-lined rotisserie in his kitchen back in the old Morrow Mill large enough to cook a small goat, noticed me one evening there sawing away on a block of cheese, and hollered at me in admonishment: "Let the knife do the work, Bland, let the knife do the work."

Every man and woman recoiled as Fred brought out the pig tongue's cubed meat on a cutting board, with a small bowl of sauce, though everyone out of obligation took a cube. He knew he was peddling a delicacy.

"Just think what all it's been licking," someone said, resisting.

"Oh, hell. Go on, get you some." Everyone did indeed get them *some*, relished it, and the tongue was gone in four minutes flat.

Wildcat Creek Joe started showing up with pecks, then great sacks of oysters that he brought up from the Carolina coast. He said he would leave the cooking to someone else.

The fine artisanal woodwright Jim Byrum stepped in. "I want to eat something," he would always say, "that slept in the ocean last night." (Core Sound would have to stand in for the Atlantic, regarding these oysters and that desire.) So he found a big quarter-inch-thick steel plate and laid it over the top of one of the fire barrels (as captain of them, I authorized this) and piled it high with oysters and roasted them.

Only Thomas sat this particular feast out.

"I ate one once," he said without elaboration, "and it worked."

One night a two-ton farm truck full of shelled corn was pulled up under the pole barn, and a couple climbed up onto it about three in the morning and dove in.

"Come on in, Thomas," one of them said.

Thomas laughed but stayed put below the truck and talked about the fun he and his pals had had when they were boys and the wheat came in at his family's farm. He said they tied the bottoms of their pants legs tight and then filled their britches with threshed wheat so their legs and girths were bulging and the boys were twice or even thrice as big as normal. Taking wide side-to-side steps like he might not have in thirty-five years, Thomas proclaimed, laughing: "We were the Wheat Men!"

There were other odd nights to remember: one night when a downpour drove the entire cooking operation over to Charles's dairy, and toward dawn Charles walked into his milking parlor and found a man and a woman up underneath his cows drinking milk straight out of their teats. The night a man whapped a woman on her thigh with a shovel when she gave him the cold shoulder and drew her righteous anger. The night a fellow from Raleigh, whom few knew, wandered through the flock of dairymen talking voodoo, and the night someone accidentally tipped an open cooker and sent sixteen pork shoulders rolling into the dirt—they had to be hosed down well before being put back onto the cooker, as if the incident had never happened.

When time got late, men napped in their pickup trucks or in aluminum chairs near the fires. Whoever's child was along usually slept in the hay toward the back of the barn, where there were half a dozen stalls and always a calf or two.

And when enough of the first light came and gently lit the mist in the bottoms down below, a little cloud forming and rising from a farm pond a half a mile away, the talk between those still barely awake was about gambling a nickel on where the sun would rise.

"Thomas," Fred always asked, "you think it'll come up to the right or left of the Snipes's silos?"

"To the right."

"Well, I'll take the left, then."

Thomas, the dairyman, far more often than not won the bet.

The real miracle was the deep spirit and love of the land that infused us all at planting time and again at harvest and at Christmas. We were barbequeing pigs to help raise money to oppose the creation of a reservoir and the flooding of Teer, in the heart of the Cane Creek–Bingham Township community. Though we lost that fight and have not had those big cooks for nearly forty years, sweet was the use of adversity that brought us together two dozen times or so over those years, that helped our advocates win environmental concessions for the protective good of the Cane Creek Lake that would come and its watershed, that cohered the communities of Bingham Township and brought us an extra measure of communion and good cheer, which for a few moments reigned over the chaotic jangle of the world beyond Bingham Township. In far more recent years, too, that spirit has restirred in the heart of our township, our membership, which as Preserve Rural Orange has helped fend off a second airport and any number of other serious nuisances, such as are often visited upon sparsely populated rural lands.

Cars streamed into the gravel drive up to the pole barn all morning long after the night of the Christmas cook, folks coming to pick up their pork. They each got a shoulder in a cardboard soda-case flat with tinfoil over the top, along with a mayonnaise bottle of homemade barbeque sauce conjured up by Thomas's wife, Evelyn, and famous throughout Bingham, the meat beneath the tinfoil still hot and *so* very aromatic.

A carol, then, for Clover Garden and Cane Creek and Orange Grove, and for Merry Oaks and Friendship and New Hill, for Eagle Rock and Bahama and Stem, for Cedar Grove and Hurdle Mills, and for all the scores of communities, named and unnamed, with their old stores like Lewis Allen's where I met Ann anew, and the farmlands and mixed forests in the far reaches of Orange and Durham and Wake Counties—miles beyond the Triangle's growing and merging metropolis, each little village and crossroads working, in the great agrarian poet Wendell Berry's words: "At holding local soil and local memory in place."

Let them all live on for many a Christmas yet to come, we pray. Even though we may wonder (and wondering makes us love them even more) if, like the now-drowned village of Teer, all these country communities we love so might well be just as ephemeral as the great rushing swarms of sparks swirling up out of the fire barrels into the night sky over our red-clay hillsides, where cord after cord of oak and hickory got used up, but not a scrap, not a splinter, ever went to waste.

Windflowers

Acknowledgments

The rolling terrain of the upper Haw River Valley has long been settled, and we deeply appreciate Mark Simpson-Vos of the University of North Carolina Press for helping us focus this work on our small portion of it. I am also indebted to Orange County (NC) register of deeds Mark Chilton for meeting with me and loaning me his extraordinary history *The Land Grant Atlas of Old Orange County, Volume II, The Saxapahaw Old Fields* (2012). Emily Bingham in her book *My Old Kentucky Home* (2022) describes her Orange County forebears (whose name lasts on our township and on a UNC–Chapel Hill classroom building on Polk Place), particularly Robert Hall Bingham and Robert Worth Bingham, as they were, and she holds them accountable for what they did. Journalist Ben Steelman's detailed biographical portraits of these two men appear in the *Dictionary of North Carolina Biography*, online at ncpedia.org. Many years ago, the *Spectator* of Raleigh let me write about the Clover Garden world; both the *Spectator* and the *Independent Weekly* (Durham) gave me room for tales of the Piedmont's hound-dog world, and my good friend the late Stephen March covered and shot coonhound events in Candor for the *Indy*; Stephen also joined me in covering draft horses at the North Carolina State Fair for the *Independent Weekly*.

Dr. Eric Schopler of UNC's TEACCH autistic children's program saved, named, and displayed Simpson's Owl for decades. The Schopler family—Eric, Miggie, Bobby, Tommy, and Susie—have been integral to our family's life in Clover Garden for half a century.

Dr. Wyndell Merritt, son of Cap'n Eben Merritt, at the request of Wyndell's and our friend D. G. Martin, sent me a clipping of writer Walter Carroll's "The Sound of Baying Dogs: A Hunt with Eben Merritt," a 1951 news feature from the *Durham Morning Herald* about nighttime coon hunting. Haywood County (NC) attorney Frank G. Queen took the time to teach me how to do the title search for what has become our lifelong home. Roger Kirkman, Bobby Schopler, and the Paul Green Foundation's Georgann Eubanks all helped with the tale of sculptor William Emsley Hipp III and his time at the old White Cross School in the 1970s and early 1980s. Pulitzer Prize–winning poet Henry Taylor graciously allowed us to use lines from his poem "An Afternoon of Pocket Billiards" to introduce my essay "Pool," which first appeared in *PineStraw Magazine* (Southern Pines, NC).

My maternal grandparents—Evelyn Moore Spruill Page and Julius Andrews Page Sr.—gave my mother, sisters, and me so many wonderful summer nights on their East Franklin Street porch, and my eternal thanks go to my grandmother for her gorgeous benedictions on all those evenings. Isa Cheren and Bill Garlick have been great hilltop neighbors for twenty-five years, and it was Bill who got us into boatbuilding. Of the core four Red Clay Ramblers (Clay Buckner, Chris Frank, Jack Herrick, and myself), my fellow three have for almost forty years given me the best reasons in the world, musical and otherwise, to ride up and down the road to Jack's a thousand times or more, as have drummers Rob Ladd and Ed Butler and banjo players Mark Roberts, Rick Good, and Don Lewis.

To the late Jake Mills go my endless friendship and deepest gratitude for so many years: *the best of all talking.*

UNC Order of the Persimmon founding member and lawyer Ted Teague of Saxapahaw unfolded for us the wonders of how that modern village has come to be. All the Admirals we know—Tom Earnhardt, David Cecelski, and David Perry—have provided us with abiding encouragements, and so have longtime friends Michael and Belinda McFee. The Morrow Mill Book Club helps keep the flame of Clover Garden community burning, as do our good friends, naturalists Carol Ann McCormick and Mark Peifer, and Laura Streitfeld, our near neighbor and the inspired soul who started Preserve Rural Orange, a model farm, forest, and community preservation nonprofit.

To all those who speak through these pages we offer our deepest thanks, to all the living and the dead.

MBS III & ACS

Index

Leechville, 83
Lee County, 21, 154
Left Bank Butchery, 127
Lewis, Carl, 129, 131–35
Lindley Mills, 125
Linville Gorge, xii
Little, Loyd, 23–24
Lloyd family, 4
Lloyd's of London, 119
Lloydtown, 4, 11
Lonely Oak Farm, 25
Long Bay, 1
Lost Cause Ball (Louisville, KY), 12
Lost Colony, The (play), 52, 154
Louisville Courier-Journal, 12
Lundstrom, Emilie, 86
Lynchburg (VA), 25

MacLean, Eliza, 127
MacNeill, Ben Dixon, 154–55
Madison (WI), 41
Mann's Chapel, 113
Mann's Harbor, 81
Manteo, 83
Maple View Farm, 10, 121–24, 140
Margaret Mills irises, 79
Marley, Bob, 111
Marlin, Andrew, 127
Marlowe, Christopher, 64
Marshallberg, 111
Matthew, book of, 123
Mayland Earth to Sky Park, 144
McCarthy, Cormac, 83
McIver Landing, 156–57
Mebane, 11, 19, 88
Mermaid Point, 160, 166
Merritt, Eben, 30–35
Merritt's (store), 30–35, 39, 56
Merry Oaks, 169
Milburnie Dam, 156
Miles, Bruce, 23–24
Million, Sherri Simpson, 119
Mills, Jerry Leath "Jake," 7, 14, 23, 34, 67, 79–82, 87, 99–100, 124, 153
Milner, Clyde, 129, 131–35

Mipso, xii, 127
Moncure, 166
Monroe, Bill, and the Bluegrass Boys, 55
Morehead-Cain Foundation (UNC), 62
Morganton, xi
Morris, Bennie, 67
Morris, Frank, 67, 70, 75
Morrison, Van, 92
Morrow, Isabel, 46
Morrow, John, 50
Morrow, Lizzie, 37
Morrow, Marvin, 39
Morrow, William, 19, 42–46, 84
Morrow family, 4, 40
Morrow Farm, 37–41, 47, 77–78, 151
Morrow Mill, 6, 12, 47, 67, 138, 153, 165–66
Mustard Seed Farm, 119

Nags Head Woods, 147
Native Americans, xii–xiii, 1
Nature Conservancy, The, 71
NC Central University, 111
NC Draft Horse and Mule Association, 24
NC State Bureau of Investigation (SBI), 36–37
NC State Fair, 24–25, 27–28
NC Wildlife Resources Commission (WRC), 153
NC Writers Network, 60
Neville's (bar), 100
New Bern, 62
New Deal, 59
New Hill, 169
New River (eastern NC), 110
New Voyage to Carolina (report), xii
New York City, 63, 82, 86, 121
New York Times, 30
NOLA Studio (New York City), 82
Nutter, Bob, and family, 122, 124

Oak Grove Café, 82, 124
Oak Island, 1
Oaks, 11, 88
Ocracoke, 144